Oral History and Ageing

Edited by Joanna Bornat
and Josie Tetley

NUMBER 9 IN
THE REPRESENTATION OF OLDER PEOPLE IN AGEING RESEARCH SERIES
THE CENTRE FOR POLICY ON AGEING AND THE CENTRE FOR AGEING AND BIOGRAPHICAL STUDIES AT THE OPEN UNIVERSITY

The Open University

First published in 2010
by the Centre for Policy on Ageing
25–31 Ironmonger Row
London EC1V 3QP
Tel: +44 (0)20 7553 6500
Fax: +44 (0)20 7553 6501
Email: cpa@cpa.org.uk
Website: www.cpa.org.uk
Registered charity no 207163

© 2010 Centre for Policy on Ageing
British Library Cataloguing in Publication Data
A catalogue record for this book is available from the British Library
ISBN 978-1-901097-16-0

The Representation of Older People in Ageing Research Series is based on
seminars organised by the Centre for Ageing and Biographical Studies,
Faculty of Health and Social Care, the Open University, and the Centre for
Policy on Ageing. The papers in this volume have been revised since the
seminar took place.

Titles in the series:

Biographical Interviews: The Link Between Research and Practice, edited by
   Joanna Bornat (No 1)

*Involving Older People in Research: 'An Amateur Doing the Work of a
   Professional?',* edited by Sheila Peace (No 2)

Writing Old Age, edited by Julia Johnson (No 3)

Everyday Living in Later Life, edited by Bill Bytheway (No 4)

Recruitment and Sampling: Qualitative Research with Older People, edited
   by Caroline Holland (No 5)

Making Observations: The Potential of Observation Methods for Gerontology,
   edited by Andrew Clark (No 6)

Language and Later Life: Issues, Methods and Representations, edited by
   Rebecca L. Jones and John Percival (No 7)

Researching Age and Multiple Discrimination, edited by Richard Ward and
   Bill Bytheway (No 8)

Printed in the United Kingdom by Henry Ling Limited,
at the Dorset Press, Dorchester DT1 1HD

CONTENTS

1   **INTRODUCTION**   1

JOANNA BORNAT AND JOSIE TETLEY

2   **TRANSNATIONAL FAMILIES, AGEING AND**   11
        REALISING DREAMS OF HOME

PAUL THOMPSON

3   **REMEMBERING IN LATER LIFE**   26
        Some lessons from oral history

ALISTAIR THOMSON

4   **SEX, LIVES AND VIDEOTAPE**   43
        Oral history group work and older adult
        education groups

GRAHAM SMITH

5   **EXPERIENCE SHARED AND VALUED**   57
        Creative development of personal and
        community memory

PAM SCHWEITZER

About the Authors   78

INTRODUCTION

JOANNA BORNAT AND JOSIE TETLEY

The papers included in this collection are from the ninth in a series of seminars exploring the representation of older people in ageing research, held by the Centre for Ageing and Biographical Studies and hosted by the Centre for Policy in Ageing. Previous seminars had focused on biographical interviews, involving older people in research, language and later life, recruitment and sampling, everyday living, age discrimination, writing old age and observation.

'Oral History and Ageing' aimed at bringing together people whose work and interests would appear to be linked: oral historians and gerontologists. Four oral historians, Paul Thompson, Alistair Thomson, Graham Smith and Pam Schweitzer, each known for their unique contribution to researching and representing the past by drawing on individual experience were invited to reflect on old age and ageing in their work.

Oral history and gerontology have had a rarely spoken relationship over the years. In the UK, though the Oral History Society and the British Society of Gerontology have shared almost the same 40 years since they originated, the *Oral History Journal* celebrates its 40th birthday in 2009 and the British Society of Gerontology will have its own 40th in 2011, there have been few acknowledgements of each other's existence. Yet the links between the two should be obvious primarily because each has an interest in older people. For the oral historian, older people are the key to the past, as witnesses they speak it, reconstruct it and, sometimes are its inventors, its authors. Gerontologists also talk to older people, though more often, perhaps, they tend to observe them and those who are close to them: their carers, friends, practitioners and spokespersons. For both gerontology and oral history, the interview is a key research tool, both focus on remembering and both show concern for issues raised by participation, ownership and the presentation of the outcomes of their engagement with the lives of older people.

Evidence that there is a basis for mutuality amongst gerontologists and oral historians is apparent from delving into the very first issues of *Oral History*. Here, one of the founders of oral history in the UK, George Ewart Evans, talks about interviewing East Anglian agricultural workers in the 1960s and we can see an awareness of the older person as participant in a joint endeavour. In his writing he reveals himself to be both a keen and prescient observer:

> But I believe that there are two aspects that can give us tremendous confidence in an interview. The first is this: the conviction that you are doing something for your informant as well as for your own purpose ... At this time most of the older generation have been shunted into the scrapyard. They feel they have lost most of their occupational skills. These have become obsolete they can no longer transmit them as they did in the former generation ... once the old people have grasped what you are about they realise ... that they have been taken back into the social family, not as temporary superannuated members but as people who can make a real contribution to social tradition. So willy-nilly we are taking part in a social therapy even if we do not realise it. It is in this setting I maintain that you will get your best results.
>
> (Evans 1972: 70)

Participation by older people has, since those early times, been noted by oral historians in the context of discussions of reminiscence and sometimes in relation to questions of community, composure, identity and forgetting. However, an understanding of what it means to become old, the generational and generational issues of being old and even the socio-economic characteristics and gendered nature of old age has tended to be overlooked by oral historians.

For their part, gerontologists, with few exceptions (notably Elder 1974; Riley 1987) tended to neglect the temporal contexts in which people have aged, the implications of local, national and world events on their ageing. What people choose to remember and why and what part stories play in the ways in which people construct their old age and relationships in old age have, with the language of biography and narrative, come to feature much more in the pages of a journal like *Ageing & Society* and at conferences of the British Society of Gerontology. A search through back issues of the journal and reviews of conference proceedings illustrates this. See for example Harrison 1983; Kohli 1988; Gubrium and Holstein 1999; Bytheway 2009 amongst others.

Awareness that the two disciplines tend to exist in parallel universes (Bornat 2001) and that cross-fertilisation between oral historians and gerontologists would be of mutual benefit was a key motivation to organise a seminar on 'Oral history and ageing' since, though they share these interests, there have been few occasions when oral historians and gerontologists have come together to examine and reflect on issues of mutual interest. A brief excursion into the history of links between the two will illustrate this point.

As early as 1981, a conference on life history and ageing held in London was organised by the gerontologist, Malcolm Johnson, then at the Policy Studies Institute, and Joanna Bornat, oral historian and at the time adult education officer at the Education Department of the charity Help the Aged. This was followed by an Oral History Society conference on oral history and reminiscence, held in 1983 at what later became the University of Central Lancashire. Papers from this were published in 1993 (Bornat 1993). These developments had been preceded by research which had opened up possibilities for collaborative work of a distinctively creative type.

Malcolm Johnson was an early advocate for what later came to be known as biographical approaches to understanding ageing in an article, 'That was your life' (Johnson 1976). Here he argued that to be able to respond sensitively and appropriately to the needs of an older person means knowing what experiences they have lived through and what is important to them in their life story. At about the same time, Peter Coleman, a psychologist with an interest in reminiscence, had begun publishing from his PhD research. His interest lay in understanding older people's inner lives through their accounts of past experience (1974) but when he later came to publish a book based on his research, the influence of cohort experiences of war and

3

unemployment and the times they had lived through was strongly evident in his analysis and theorising (1986). These first UK expositions of biographical approaches were undoubtedly inspired by the work of Robert Butler, a US psychiatrist with an interest in ageing who, in 1963, had published a paper advocating use of life review as a helpful intervention in encounters with older people who were in some way troubled (Butler 1963). As has been pointed out since, that paper was to be a landmark (Dobrof 1984) and even today (2009) a Google search shows 1129 citations in academic journals. Drawing on his experiences as principal investigator into the mental health of older people living in the community he had argued against the assumption common amongst psychologists and psychiatrists that talk of the past, reminiscence, was a sign of pathology, of mental deterioration. Those who followed his lead in the US and UK helped to shift reminiscence from being studied for its function, pattern and content to becoming an activity which might be deliberately encouraged and established as beneficial and, unavoidably, participatory.

Butler's role in championing life review was undoubtedly enhanced by his reputation as an engaged and outspoken critic of ageist policies in US health care and social policy. His critique of government policies, drawing on evidence as to the social, political and psychological determinants of late life marginalisation, *Why Survive? Being Old in America* (1975) won a Pulitzer Prize for non-fiction within a year of its publication. In the book, chapter 14, 'Growing Old Absurd' includes, 'The tendency toward life review' amongst 10 'special characteristics of later life' which counter stereotypical 'placing (of) the old … in prescribed roles' (1975: 409).

Butler's focus on inequalities and the positive contribution of encouraging people to remember, fed into developments in the UK which were to bring oral historians and gerontologists together working on practical projects. In the late 1970s, an architect working for the then Department of Health and Social Services, Mick Kemp, had developed a series of sounds and images which he called 'Reminiscence Aids'. Later to be taken up and published as *Recall* by Help the Aged Education Department, these tape-slide sequences were to make a mark on care relationships in formal and informal settings (Bornat 2010) particularly when espoused by sensitive practitioners (Adams 1986). *Recall* legitimised and reversed attitudes to an activity that had previously been disregarded as valueless at best, demeaning at worst. Linked with community-based oral history projects, evidence that older people's remembering had value not just for individuals but for groups and for the communities where they lived, had begun to change the nature of oral history too, as the first edition of Thompson's *Voice of the Past* (1978) was already able to demonstrate. Armed with the evidence of programmes and materials such as *Recall,* oral history soon became the province of community activists and promoters of the welfare of older people run by organisations such as Centreprise in Hackney and QueenSpark in Brighton. More recently such activity has become a central part of funded oral history making through what might now be called the 'heritage industry' with Heritage Lottery alone having spent £49M on oral history projects by 2007 (Thomson 2008: 103).

'Oral History and Ageing' was organised as an opportunity to reflect in the company of some leading UK oral historians on what their common and shared interests and concerns might be. The four people who were invited to speak have all shown consistent interest and awareness of the implications of age and ageing in their work. Paul Thompson made an early foray into this area with his jointly authored study, *'I don't feel old': the experience of later life* (Thompson *et al.* 1990). This drew on three sets of data, published autobiography, archived interviews and a set of specially generated interviews, to explore how people feel about ageing and being old. Al Thomson's *Anzac Memories* (1994) a study of the changing significance of memories of the Anzac legend in Australian society, deliberately focused on meaning and reflection in late life in his interviews with four very old ex-combatants. Graham Smith has a long-standing interest in community history making and in oral history in health and social care (Smith and Jackson 1999). The dynamics of oral history making and the part played by memory in the lives of older women, in a town like Dundee where he carried out his PhD research proved an early focus for him. Pam Schweitzer has worked for close on thirty years as a theatre director drawing on the words of older people and directing them, and younger people, in productions which she has staged in London, the UK and farther afield. At the time of the seminar her book, *Reminiscence Theatre: Making Theatre from Memories,* was about to be published (Schweitzer 2007).

Each of the four presenters was asked to look back on their work in relation to ageing for an audience principally comprising gerontologists. Given their very different backgrounds contributions to the development of oral history work, each illustrates different perspectives and ways of working, reflecting autobiographically at times. The seminar was to be memorable for many reasons but principally because it brought together (unfortunately without Pam Schweitzer being actually present her paper being read in her absence) key oral historians, one of whom, Al Thomson, would shortly be returning to his native Australia after a celebrated career in oral history and community history in the UK.

In terms of methodological innovations in ageing research the four papers each make a distinctive contribution, presenting different approaches to oral history work. Thus the first paper by Paul Thompson demonstrates how oral history with individuals can be linked to enhance our understanding of particular events or broader periods of history. The value of this way of working has been demonstrated by the American oral historian Studs Terkel who conducted interviews and presented narrative accounts to highlight people's lived experiences of World War II and the Great Depression in relation to the notion of the American Dream (Terkel 1970; 1981; 1985).

Paul Thompson explores older people's experiences of migration from Jamaica to North America and UK. By looking across and comparing distinctively different individual stories he identifies the strategies, developed through familial and community networks of support, which enabled people to survive in the sometimes hostile environments in which they found themselves. Aspirations to return to home, rooted in the landscapes of childhood sustained them, but now, a life time away has resulted in feelings of a mixed identity which complicates decisions about where to grow old.

Whilst the four papers in this collection demonstrate the positive contribution that oral history can bring to our understanding of the past, traditional historians have often criticised this way of working,

6

questioning the reliability and validity of historical accounts developed from subjective stories and unreliable memories (Smith 2008). In response, Alistair Thomson's paper tackles this issue directly, focusing on the experience of remembering World War I soldiering and the life writing of a woman who took up the opportunity to become a 'Ten Pound Pom', trying out life in Australia when young. In drawing on these two interviews with people at different life stages, he demonstrates how culture, relationships and people's motivations to recall and talk about past events, not memory itself, most significantly shape and influence the stories that people tell in late life.

Graham Smith and Pam Schweitzer demonstrate the effect of group and social processes on recall and storytelling in oral history work. Graham Smith specifically demonstrates how different methods can promote 'transactive' remembering as a group works together to share stories and experiences of a particular period of time or event. Wegner *et al.* (1991) argue that using transactive processes are particularly valuable as a group memory system can aid in the recall of more information than any one individual can. However, Graham Smith notes that oral historians have not necessarily favoured group remembering as a method of data collection. His paper is therefore of interest for the insights he draws on from using two methods, the 'free for all' and 'taking turns'. Drawing on examples from group interviews he explores older people's experiences of life and work in Dundee. Following on from this Pam Schweitzer's paper reflects on her work with reminiscence theatre and how in her experience sharing memories in groups enables people to identify and develop a sense of community. By sharing memories and stories in interviews people were able to see how their individual experiences related to others in group. Through this they were able to recognise the value of their everyday lives and experiences. Pam's paper, however, argues the value of going beyond the individual and group. Turning group memories and stories into arts based outputs such as plays, books and exhibitions has enabled the stories to be shared in positive and therapeutic ways across generations and community groups. She ends on a critically reflective note as she describes her reactions to having the tables turned on her in a recent oral history interview.

The chapters which follow illustrate four very different approaches within an oral history tradition, yet each has resonance and relevance for gerontologists. The themed approach taken by Paul Thompson, drawing out commonalities in family and community life amongst a sample of interviewees, contrasts with Al Thomson's use, in this case, of the single interview. Different again are Graham Smith's and Pam Schweitzer's use of the group interview, controversial in oral history, each having differently designed outcomes. For all four, the foregrounding of older people's life experience is at the heart of the interview relationship. And, as important, their participation is viewed as a joint enterprise, a process to be shared as much as possible from first encounter to final production.

Our aim, in presenting this collection, is to stimulate further discussions and opportunities to share research approaches and findings amongst oral historians and gerontologists in the hope that creative research partnerships may ensue in the future.

REFERENCES

Adams, J. (1986) 'Anamnesis in dementia: Restoring a personal history', *Geriatric Nursing,* September/October, 25–27.

Bornat, J. (1993) *Reminiscence Reviewed: Perspectives, Evaluations, Achievements.* Buckingham: Open University Press.

Bornat, J. (2001) 'Reminiscence and oral history: Parallel universes or shared endeavour?', *Ageing & Society*, 21(2), 219–241.

Bornat, J. (2010) 'Remembering as the politics of later life', in D. Ritchie (ed.) *The Oxford Handbook to Oral History.* New York: Oxford University Press.

Butler, R.N. (1963) 'The life review: An interpretation of reminiscence in the aged', *Psychiatry*, 26, 65–76.

Butler, R.N. (1975) *Why Survive: Being Old in America.* New York: Harper & Row.

Bytheway, B. (2009) 'Writing about birthdays and the passage of time', *Ageing & Society*, 29(6), 883–901.

Coleman, P. (1974) 'Measuring reminiscence characteristics from conversation as adaptive features of old age', *International Journal of Aging and Human Development*, 5(3), 281–294.

Coleman, P. (1986) *Ageing and Reminiscence Processes: Social and Clinical Implications*. Chichester: Wiley.

Dobrof, R. (1984) 'Introduction: A time for reclaiming the past', in M. Kaminsky (ed.) *The Uses of Reminiscence: New Ways of Working with Older Adults*. New York: The Haworth Press.

Elder, G.H. (1974) *Children of the Great Depression*. Chicago: University of Chicago Press.

Evans, G.E. (1972) 'Approaches to interviewing', *Oral History*, 1(4), 56–71.

Gubrium, J.F. and Holstein, J.A. (1999) 'The nursing home as a discursive anchor for the ageing body', *Ageing & Society*, 19(5), 519–538.

Harrison, J. (1983) 'Women and ageing: Experience and implications', *Ageing & Society*, 3(2), 209–235.

Johnson, M. (1976) 'That was your life: A biographical approach to later life', in J.M.A. Munnichs and W.J.A. van den Heuvel (eds) *Dependency and Interdependency in Old Age*. The Hague, Netherlands: Martinus Nijhoff, pp. 147–161.

Kohli, M. (1988) 'Ageing as a challenge for Sociological Theory', *Ageing & Society*, 8(4), 367–394.

Riley, M.W. (1987) 'On the significance of age in sociology', *American Sociological Review*, 52, 1–14.

Schweitzer, P. (2007) *Reminiscence Theatre: Making Theatre from Memories*. London: Jessica Kingsley.

Smith, G. (2008) The making of oral history: Sections 1–2. http://www.history.ac.uk/makinghistory/resources/articles/oral_hi story.html (last accessed 1st of September 2009)

Smith, G. and Jackson, P. (1999) 'Narrating the nation: The "imagined community" of Ukrainians in Bradford', *Journal of Historical Geography*, 25(3), 367–387.

Terkel, S. (1970) *Hard Times: An Oral History of the Great Depression*. London: Allen Lane, The Penguin Press.

Terkel, S. (1981) *American Dreams: Lost and Found*. London: Hodder and Stoughton.

Terkel, S. (1985) *'The Good War': An Oral History of World War Two*. London: Hamish Hamilton.

Thompson, P. (1978) *The Voice of the Past*, third edn 2000. Oxford: Oxford University Press.

Thompson, P., Itzin, C. and Abendstern, M. (1990) *I Don't Feel Old: The Experience of Later Life*. Oxford: Oxford University Press.

Thomson, A. (1994) *Anzac Memories: Living with the Legend*. Oxford: Oxford University Press.

Thomson, A. (2008) 'Oral history and community history in Britain: Personal and critical reflections on twenty-five years of continuity and change', *Oral History*, 36(1), 95–104.

Wegner, R., Erber, R. and Raymond, P. (1991) 'Transactive memory in close relationships', *Journal of Personality and Psychology*, 61(6), 923–929.

2

TRANSNATIONAL FAMILIES, AGEING AND REALISING DREAMS OF HOME

PAUL THOMPSON

For very many migrants, wherever they have come from or to, getting older is associated with dreams of returning to their original homeland for their years of retirement. But realising such dreams can bring paradoxical consequences. In their years away, the migrants' own sense of identity may have taken a new shape, and the homeland itself may have radically changed. My purpose here is to look at these changes through the experiences of the Jamaican migrants whom Elaine Bauer and I have interviewed. For our book *Jamaican Hands Across the Atlantic* (2006), we carried out over a hundred life story interviews with members of 45 transnational Jamaican families who have kin in North America and Britain as well as Jamaica. The great majority of those we interviewed had hopes of returning to Jamaica, and some had realised their dream. In this talk I discuss how migrants developed an idealised view of their homeland, and how returning proved a demanding social struggle which could change their fundamental identity at the end of their lives.

For these interviews, we aimed to get a proper range and breadth of the different kinds of experience. There are successful middle class professional Jamaicans and there are poor Jamaicans on welfare, and we wanted to capture that diversity. So we set up a rough quota, which was very crude – manual and non manual, men, women and age – and we built around that. There were no samples we could have used in the different countries so initially we used networks. But we found the difficulty was that if you went through networks you got fewer of the less successful people. Not always. A couple of family networks produced some very poor people, but on the whole there was a tendency towards the more successful. So we tried to balance that out by literally finding people. For example we obtained one very interesting interview, when we were getting off a subway train in

New York and there was a man selling oils and other concoctions by the exit. I looked at him and I thought he would talk – and he did. Or we might get talking to a taxi-driver, and then ask for an interview.

I have used that kind of approach before, even in finding interviews for my first oral history project in the early 1970s, 'The Edwardians'. There was a man living under a pseudonym who was picked up on a park bench in London, and turned out to be a runaway seaman. But I think making the most of chance encounters is really important with this kind of research, because projects with migrants usually choose interviewees overwhelmingly through recommend-ations and networks, so they can easily suffer from this push towards the more successful end of the migrant experience. I think even so with our own project we probably got too favourable an impression of the Jamaican experience in Canada, precisely because it was there where we had the initial advantage of the strongest network contacts.

We realised this when we tried to compare statistics about Jamaicans who had gone to the different countries. Making comparisons is very difficult because each national set is collected on a different basis. But it does look from the figures as if Jamaicans are among the bottom group of migrants to Canada, while they are not among the poorest groups in either Britain or the United States. In Britain there is a very sharp difference between the success of Caribbean women that is comparable with that of white women, and Caribbean men who are much less successful. In the United States Jamaicans are again not the bottom group and they have an image of being hard-working and committed to education, which is frequently contrasted with the indigenous black population. But while it is clearly useful to compare statistical evidence with such a project on migrants, this does not lead us towards a sample. Even national figures of migrants are often highly inaccurate, precisely because so many migrants are 'illegals' without proper visas. Hence there is no way you could sample transnational families. So there is no choice but to work in a fairly primitive way. That's what we did. But I think that nevertheless we have got a very interesting range of experience.

A second issue is to ask how far we may have influenced these interviews ourselves. For roughly half of the interviews both of us were present, while the remainder were recorded separately by Elaine or Paul. Given our very different social images, Elaine a younger black Jamaican-Canadian woman and Paul an older white Englishman, whoever led the interview could have had a significant influence in shaping the testimonies, and we looked carefully to see how far this was so. The really important difference seemed to be in the setting up of the interview, which Elaine was able to achieve much more easily and quickly than Paul – indeed he was sometimes given a prolonged grilling before starting. In the interviews, on the other hand, it seems that the importance of these differences in social position quickly faded. We both followed the same life story format which we had worked out together, and although Elaine's style is a little more conversational, there are no obvious differences in the broad content of the interviews. Not only is the broad coverage the same, but we equally often recorded men and women who used many *patois* phrases; and we were each as often told about 'outside' children, or illegal activities, or experiences of racism. The really striking differences are much more between the interviewees themselves. Thus some would give brief responses, while others would articulate their memories at length or shape some of their story according to their religious beliefs – which could be with either of us. We have also been able to compare our recorded material with many informal conversations with migrant Jamaicans, visiting families, travelling round Jamaica in route taxis and so on. All this gives us confidence in its quality as evidence. So what did we learn about migrant dreams and their realisation?

THE LANDSCAPE AND THE DREAM

One point that we noticed was that when migrants talked about the Jamaican countryside and landscape, it was usually different from Jamaicans who had stayed in Jamaica, who typically spoke of the land in a much more factual way. I'm not saying everybody did. They talked about using land, building a house or farming. But migrants could be quite lyrical in their descriptions.

Thus when we interviewed Selvin Green[1] he was working as a welder in a computer parts factory in Battersea. Born into a skilled family with little land, he was brought up by his grandmother in the beautiful mountain countryside of eastern Jamaica. Since migrating to England, before we interviewed him he had already been back once to Jamaica, and he has gone back since, permanently. However it is interesting that earlier in his interview he recalls how glad he was as a teenager to move to Kingston, seeing the city as an escape from a monotonous fate: 'Oh, it was great! When I was in Kingston, one is like you're in heaven! Yes, it was great! Because I'm always at work ... because I didn't want to work in the fields, in the cane fields ... I hate that ... Kingston is the big bright lights, and everything is there.'

Nevertheless by the time we interviewed him in middle life in London, his view had become transformed. When he spoke of the Jamaican landscape, it was now in terms of observing rather than doing, as an environmentally sensitive townsman, rather than as a practical farmer or smallholder. And he was drawn to return again to 'my home' with the passion of a nature-lover. What draws him so powerfully is:

> The lifestyle, the place, the beauty. The simplicity of life. I to go out the back and pick a lettuce, just off the real land grown on. I want to pick orange. I want to hear the birds. I want to see the coconuts, I want to hear the wind blow between it ... I want to see the bees fly up to the flowers, and I want to stand there, because I used to do that, and look at it taking the nectar from the flowers, you know?

> Cos I used to do that. I used to watch, I used to get disciplined for it. When I'm going down to the stream to get water ... That's like you see a bird fly in the tree, and it make a sound, a whistle: when you look, you see another one fly, come along, and some communication going on between those two bird. These are the things I like.

---

[1] We gave people the option of being called by their real name or pseudonyms, and Selvin chose his real name.

Now this image of the Caribbean as a tropical paradise is very widespread. It is common enough in travel literature. So it is not peculiar to black West Indians, but for them it can be a great deal more important, for such images are more likely to shape their later life dreams. Over half of the people we interviewed are still hoping to return to Jamaica. Let us take, for example, Ted Oliver, whom we interviewed outside Toronto. He has done well as a migrant, and become very integrated, so you would not think he would be especially keen to leave Canada to go back to Jamaica. But he lives with this dream.

Today Ted Oliver is a truck driver, and he lives comfortably in Canada with his white wife Candy and their two children in the three-bedroom house they have bought in a Toronto suburb. They chose this suburb because it has a good school. Ted has been in Canada since he was twenty, and Candy comes from a Canadian farm family. A crucial bond between them has been that they were both brought up by their grandparents: despite such different ethnic origins, he feels that 'we have the same background'. Ted now sees his own identity as mixed – 'I'm part of Jamaica, I'm part of Canada' – and they have brought up the children to enjoy both cultures, taking them on holidays to Jamaica and introducing them to relatives there. They play both Jamaican and American music, and they cook a mixture of Italian and Jamaican food, with Jamaican most Sundays: 'yam, fried plantain, ackee and saltfish, callaloo'. But Ted's ultimate dream is not of more success and more mixing in Canada. It is of return. 'I still have my grandfather land.' He would like to build his new family a house on this family land back in Jamaica, in the Trelawney hills where he grew up, and with Candy this has become a shared vision for their future lives together:

My wife now, she's this type of person who likes to move. She have this type of feeling, 'Oh yes, let's go to Jamaica and live in the woods.' Up to this morning we were travelling on the highway, she said, 'Why you wanna live in this mess?' ... Because the first place I take her in Jamaica, in the mountain, and take her in Cockpit mountain, and she loved it. First when I take her, I went to – they have a spring in the mountain, so we take our shoes off, they have these kind of plants in Jamaica, but they are big vines, and we take it and wrap it round her feet, tie it up ... We walk across the canefield, we go to the spring and drink water, catch the water coming up from the ground, drink it. Go in the mountain, see the difference. She love that. ... She said to me this morning, 'Let us sell the house and go and live freely.' I see that. I can match myself to that.

Ted is in his fifties. He sees his 'grandfather land' as the place to build his new house, but this might prove his first difficulty. There is a system in Jamaica of family land which is held or always was held in the past on a purely oral basis, there were no legal documents. It originated after the end of slavery, when there was a tremendous wish to acquire land as a security. Sometimes people held onto their slave provision plots, sometimes they bought land from former colonial estates, and there were also Baptist missions who bought up land specifically to distribute to people. The custom is for family land to be passed down to all the descendants of its original ex-slave owners on both sides – male and female – and they all have the right to use the land. They don't own bits of it, but have the right to use the land to keep animals, grow crops, and build a house. But today this is difficult because there are by now far too many potential claimants. What happens in practice is that priority is given to people who need it most, so if you are a successful migrant you are likely to be strongly discouraged and told to go and buy your own piece of land. Since the local view of land is likely to be practical rather than lyrical, Ted's dream might not prove as simple to realise as it sounds.

PREPARING TO RETURN TO JAMAICA

In the end, as we shall see, only a small number do return. Why is this? Many older migrants have come to accept, if reluctantly, that they are going to live out their lives in the land where they have settled. As the Jamaican proverb puts it, 'Where the tree falls, it lies there'.

There was also a minority who had decisively rejected the idea of returning at any point in their lives, partly because they felt they had a higher standard of living and Jamaica was too primitive. There is also fear of violence. It is striking how in some interviews we heard fantasy views of the horrors of life in Jamaica. Even a health professional, who might have known better, said, 'In Jamaica today everybody lives in a prison with locked gates, burglar alarms and bad dogs in the garden.' Now this is a mythical view: in reality Jamaica is not like that. Even the well-off people in the capital on the whole don't live behind great metal security grilles, and indeed there is less gated housing in Kingston than in London. Certainly there is serious violence, but the flavour of everyday life is much more relaxed. Possibly such mythical views can be helpful as some kind of defence against returning – against the pull to go home.

Despite all this many Jamaicans do go back. We had twelve people among our interviewees who have gone back for substantial periods, and six of them are still there. They all spoke positively about returning. When they did not stay, sometimes it was because they went before retirement and had found difficulty in getting the kind of work they hoped for: for example, if they were professionals wanting a similar job. Then there were others who had gone back to Jamaica because they thought their children would get a better education. Jamaicans think highly of the island's schools, which are much more disciplined there than here in the United Kingdom.

What are the motives of returnees who end up leaving Jamaica again? Some want higher education outside the island for their children. Another reason is some kind of family dispute: for example, one man came back from Jamaica just as a quiet way of splitting up with his wife. Lastly, the commonest reason with older people is the lack of free health care in Jamaica. The health system there is very expensive, so that it is difficult for a seriously sick returnee to stay on in Jamaica, rather than return for the mainly free health services in Britain or Canada.

This touches on another influential image that many Jamaicans have of their childhood community: the caring, of both children and the old, by neighbours. The duty to care is deeply instilled in many Jamaicans, and we were indeed impressed by how far transnational families of migrants are able to sustain these practices. In every family there were examples of children who for at least part of their lives were brought up by kin other than their parents, and in at least a quarter of the families there were parallel instances of caring for the old. As is customary in Jamaican kinship, caring was seen as a reciprocal obligation based on shared experience, rather than a purely formal duty. Thus more often than not both men and women have children with more than one partner. If the father has moved on, it is crucial that he keeps in touch and sends some financial support. If not, when he turns up in late middle age or older seeking out his children they are unlikely to be much interested. One man whom we interviewed in London is the father of eight daughters in Britain and Canada, by three or four different women, but appears to have given them no support whatsoever. Now he is seriously ill and so is his wife, but only one of his daughters is even willing to be in touch. The rest take the attitude, 'If you were not there for me when I was young and needed your help, why should I help you now?' In contrast, take the case of Louis May, who had been brought up by his grandmother. When the family in Jamaica called him in England to tell him that she had suffered a stroke, he came back immediately. 'I had to grab everything, everything, and spend the next night coming, on the plane to Jamaica. And I tell you after this stage, because the thing is that I had to lift her up like a baby … And what came back to me was what she used to do to me when I was a baby.'

Nevertheless many returnees are likely to be over-optimistic about the family support they can get in Jamaica. They are not returning to the communities of their childhood, but to more individualistic societies, in which the obligation to care – as indeed in Britain too – is felt less strongly than a generation ago. Equally important, by returning they are most likely to leave behind their closest family with whom they will have shared the most bonding experiences, and live instead among remoter kin who have much less reason to feel obligation to support them.

Most returnees, long before they finally return to Jamaica, have been making elaborate plans. Typically they have set about building a big new family house on the island. Except for those whose family had substantial land, and who can therefore easily return to live close to kin, these houses are typically in clusters on new estates. If you go to Jamaica today you can quickly see the impact of returning, because the island is peppered with the newly built houses of returnees. They tend to be close to the coastline although you find them inland on the hills as well. These houses are very extraordinary for they are typically built over long periods, not just put up in one go but are often built – partly by the family themselves – over ten or more years, so that many of them are only half finished. People often die before their houses are finished. They are big, three-storeys or more, usually with many more rooms than an ageing couple could need. The idea is that they can then have extended families to stay, so you might have ten bedrooms. Hence when completed they can be enormous. But those half-finished stand like an enormous skeleton, or even a half- ruined abbey. Returnees' houses have become a striking feature of the contemporary Jamaican landscape.

It is important to mention that these building projects may have an important negative effect for the next generation. Returnees usually finance their retirement by eventually selling their houses in London or the Midlands, which have often become valuable properties. But because there is a glut of them, and many are only half-finished, the new houses in Jamaica are not going to be easy to sell when the returnees die or decide to come back to Britain or North America. Hence in terms of the next generation this is probably a bad move, a waste of the family's assets. This may help to explain why social mobility studies have found that successful Caribbeans do not transmit their status to their children as easily as most other social groups do. One reason may be that they are taking their money out of the country and putting it into these dream houses, rather than helping to buy houses for their own children.

THE STRUGGLE TO SETTLE IN

The decision to return builds on old dreams and childhood memories, but to succeed it has to be tackled as a new project. Most migrants have kept in touch with family in Jamaica by letter and phone over the years, and most go back from time to time on holiday. One family whom we interviewed in New York has a regular custom of four-way transnational phone chatting on Sunday mornings, talking about traditional Jamaican themes like church or cooking ackee and salt fish. Several of the wealthier families have also held grand re-unions of extended family in hotels in Jamaica, usually to celebrate a wedding or special birthday.

Once returning migrants reach Jamaica they are likely to be taken by surprise by the difficulties they face in settling back into their local communities. These difficulties come from both sides. This can be seen from the experiences of two women, both strong characters who had become professional nurses in Britain. Women's voices are particularly important here, because while returning is usually a couple enterprise, typically the men lead in building the house and the women in building bridges with the local churches and community.

Winnie Busfield had worked as a hospital nurse in Yorkshire. She told us that for her 'the major part of getting back into the system is over', but nevertheless, re-integrating had been hard:

> It was difficult at first. Very very difficult. Certainly was very hard. As if the whole custom had changed. People attitude was rougher, not like most of the people I knew when I was small – they're all gone to foreign. So it was a whole generation with the new ideas, more disrespectful to adults, and so forth, so it was hard. But I am a very determined person, I overcome all those. ... I am now well into the system. I fight my way into the system! Even the churches! Oh yes! Barriers in the churches.

Vivia Perrin has also been a professional nurse, and in London she has been a church-goer and community activist, including fostering children and victim support. She has returned in that spirit – 'for me, coming back, I needed that purpose' – but she has no illusions that succeeding as a returnee is easy. She reflected on how she has watched too many others fail:

> If they were from Jamaica, twenty years is enough to get them into the culture of the United States, or the culture of Britain. Then they come back, but most of them come back and they have not moved Jamaica on. Somewhere they left it. So a lot of them are disappointed, a lot of them are disheartened. And a lot of the people here, I've seen a big number going back to

Britain. I don't know what it is going to do for them, because they have sold their homes, they have severed their ties with the church, with their communities, and the money they bring here, to build a house that they've got here, they cannot resell at a price to go back and buy again.

That is very true. One couple we interviewed had bought a lovely house in Jamaica – up on a hill overlooking the sea – but because of illness they are now back in a one-bedroom council flat in West London. The contrast could not be more striking. It is certainly true, that if you can't make it as a returnee you are likely to suffer a big drop in your position.

Vivia says that returnees need 'a network of support', and many are disappointed not to get that from their families: 'the biggest complaint you have from returning residents is from families'. This is partly because the family members in Jamaica are typically not their immediate family (who have not returned with them), but may be quite distant kin who, seeing them as wealthy successful migrants, are trying to get something out of them. Many people who have never left Jamaica have delusions about the wealth of those who have left, and think money is oozing out of their pockets. In fact few returnees have the resources for largesse.

Vivia advises would-be returnees to come out for four or five visits on 'fact-finding tours', checking out finances, security and so on: taking it gradually as she and her husband Albert did. She has set up a support organisation for the whole of the south of Jamaica, called the Returning Residents Groups. She has also become a local community activist, setting up a neighbourhood watch, she sits on three school boards, and is raising money to open a new local health centre, raising the money with support from the churches in Britain. She is the model re-integrating returnee, and she has thrown her energy and heart and soul into these multiple campaigns.

TWISTS IN IDENTITY

I want to finish with the issue of migrant identity and how that is related to return. Now we found great differences in the sense of identity between migrants to the United States on one hand, and to Canada and Britain on the other.

When we first went to New York to interview migrants and their children for our book, their stories in many ways echoed those we had already heard in Britain and Canada, but we were taken by surprise by one sharp difference. Almost unanimously, however materially successful, and often despite having taken American citizenship, they emphatically rejected the possibility that they had become Americans. As one woman put it, 'I'm not American. I have American citizenship, but I'm not an American. I'm a Jamaican.' But while migrants to the United States almost all saw themselves quite simply as Jamaicans, in both Britain and Canada, we found migrants more likely to describe themselves as having acquired a mixed identity, whether as 'Jamaican Canadian' or 'cosmopolitan' or in more complex ways. Take for example Josephine Buxton, now a Londoner, who speaks of her identity as a history of experiences and mixed feelings, with the biblical cadences which once suited a pastor's wife:

> I am like, I am like Moses, never forget that he was a Hebrew, even being brought up at the palace of the king. Always I am a Jamaican and a West Indian. I know that I am from Jamaica, I have so much of my old culture in me. I have adopted so many others of other country until, I think, I've lost so much of my culture too. But there is the little bit that lives there. ... that I am a Jamaican.

This is not what might be expected. There seems to be little difference in terms of overall black–white occupational inequalities between Britain, Canada and the United States: in each country the broad figures show twice as many blacks as whites unemployed, half as many as whites in professional jobs, and so on. But in the United States wage rates are highest and, in addition, West Indians are in proportion better educated and occupationally more successful than indigenous African Americans. Hence on a simple materialistic basis, Jamaicans in America should be more likely to identify with their new country. Why is this not so?

It is of course impossible to make more than suggestions to this very complex issue here. But one key reason might be how over generations both racism and reactions to it have shifted. The migrants to Britain are mostly from an older generation who came between the late 1940s and the early 1960s, before more restrictive immigration legislation was imposed. They had to fight against an unrestricted racism, especially in housing and work, but they had grown up in colonial Jamaica where whites were still on top, and were able to deal with the racism they found in Britain. Despite it, they retained a certain pride in coming to the 'Mother Country', and being British citizens. Crucially too, most migrants to Britain have spent much more of their lives away from Jamaica, so that they have had much more life experience to reshape their original identities.

Most later migrants went to the United States and Canada which both switched to more open immigration policies from the early 1970s just as entry to Britain had become much more difficult. Meanwhile there had been important changes in Jamaica over these decades. Younger migrants were leaving a Jamaica which was becoming racially more open, and its black majority population more self-confident; and thus may have been more likely to feel surprise and anger at experiencing racist discrimination in North America than the older generation had been in Britain.

But time does not help to explain the contrast in attitudes between migrants to Canada and the United States, which are almost as different as between migrants to the United States and Britain. There must have been other factors also at play. We explored the significance of culture shock on first arrival, but the stories of encountering a new climate, a new urban environment and a new society on the one hand, and of emotional loss on the other, echo down the generations, wherever the migrants went. We also asked whether there were important differences in the alienating processes of immigration: but while the interviews certainly showed how the difficulties in getting work visas kept many migrants in low paid jobs, and pushed them towards cheating the system, these were again difficulties wherever the migrants went.

It was only when we looked at differences in the forms of racism that we began to see why it might be more difficult for migrants to identify with the United States. While in Canada and also Britain the combined pressures of new laws and changed public opinion have greatly reduced open racism and discrimination, changes in practice have been much less marked in the United States. The really important distinction between migrant destinations highlighted by the interviews was the hostility of migrants to the racially segregated sociability, which they encountered especially in New York. In Jamaica they had been used to racial mixing: but as migrants they found themselves in ethnically segregated housing, with little social contact outside work between white and black, and very few mixed couple relationships. Younger migrants especially expressed anger at this, holding onto a Jamaican identity for the values as well as for the personal experiences which it symbolised.

Whether migrants have held onto a simple Jamaican identity, or developed a more complex mixed form, for returnees, the ultimate paradox is discovering an unexpected final identity. On the one hand, their difficulties in reintegrating challenge their sense of being Jamaican. On the other, they discover that the group they have most in common with are the people with whom they have lived in their country of migration, whether England or in North America. They tend to live close together and socialise together, sharing memories they hold in common. Above all, locals call them the 'English' and they can only accept that. In short, they have lost their Jamaican identity in their own homeland.

Let us conclude with the returnee experience of Winnie Busfield. Today Winnie's local friends are 'mainly through the church'. She has got over her initial surprise, after living for years as an exception in a world of white faces, that here in Jamaica, 'everywhere I go, there were all these black faces, and for a while, it took me a good while really to grasp it, that this was a black country'. She has learnt to speak patois again, and she has become a travelling missionary in Jamaica. But this very process of resettling has brought a profound change in her sense of identity. She has come to feel that she is perhaps as much English as Jamaican:

> Now, if you look at my community here, you will see that it's mainly returning residents, so that makes it much easier, because you have so much in common.... If it was all the everyday Jamaicans, I could not cope with it.... I could not

relate to somebody that I hadn't shared the same culture with for forty years. You understand? ...We go from England, so you have a lot of things in common....You know more about them [returnees] than you know about your own Jamaicans [neighbours and family], because most of your years you've spent with them....You can talk about a place in England, and they can chat about the place. Now, when I got back to Jamaica here, there is hardly any place I know.... I know more of England than Jamaica.

Now, if you have gone back straight into the heart of the community, you will have more problems. Because sometimes they call us 'foreigners', oh yes. In England we were foreigners, you come back to Jamaica, your country, you're foreigners. So you get it from both sides.

REFERENCE

Bauer, E. and Thompson, P. (2006) *Jamaican Hands Across the Atlantic.* Kingston: Ian Randle Publishers.

3

REMEMBERING IN LATER LIFE
Some lessons from oral history

ALISTAIR THOMSON

In popular culture there is a common sense that, as we get older, our memory becomes more fragile and unreliable. Critics of oral history have certainly been quick to lampoon the 'mumblings of old men' and 'old wives' tales'. But oral historians and memory researchers know that long-term memory is remarkably robust, and that age is only one of many factors – and probably not the most significant – that affects what and how we remember. Remembering is shaped by the way we seek to find language and make a story about past experience, and that process might involve particular challenges for older people when the words and storylines about experience have changed over the decades. The story we wish to recall and relate about our past will certainly be affected one way or another by the wider cultural memory – of family, community or nation – of the events we have lived through. When we recall our past life we may also be influenced by a deep-felt desire to create coherent sense about our life and a story we can live with – to achieve composure – and perhaps that desire for life review is experienced in a rather different way in later life. And we will almost always be remembering in a relationship – perhaps directly with a younger interviewer or indirectly when we speak through them to an imagined audience. The relationships within which older people remember their lives may well have a distinctive character and influence, but whatever our age the relationships for remembering will have a profound effect on the story that is told.

This paper aims to identify and explore the ways in which age, more specifically old age, is a significant factor for remembering in later life. Examples are taken from two interviews: one with a 96-year-old war veteran interviewed in 1983 (see Thomson 1994), and another with a 66-year-old 'return' migrant interviewed in 2000 (see Hammerton and Thomson 2005; Thomson 2010).

There is often a tension between ourselves and the external world and remembering – an on-going process by which we make sense of our lives. If public stories do not work we may try to find other stories or narratives that help us to achieve composure (Thomson 1994). The question is how does old age, specifically the later stages of life, fit into that model of remembering? Along with the sets of factors that affect the remembering – the personal, the social and the relational – we can also look at how those things might work differently at different life stages and distinctively in older age. Clearly relationships could influence remembering in older age. For example, we may have a particular way we tell stories to grandchildren or we might be remembering with a University of the Third Age group or we might be remembering in loneliness and struggling to find an audience to make sense of our lives.

One of the significant things about remembering events 50 years ago is that we have to negotiate a whole range of shifting cultural memories – the ones that were around at the time and ones that have happened since (Summerfield 2004). Gerontologists and reminiscence workers have produced a considerable body of research on life review that encompasses the personal sphere of remembering in later life. The suggestion is that processes of remembering and reflecting back on life differ as we get close to the end of our lives. Maybe we want to try and make sense of all that has happened, or perhaps there is more time to reflect, or simply people are being asked to do that sort of remembering work. The nature of remembering, the relationships, and the personal significance of remembering might well be different in older age. We need to isolate what is specific about older age and later life in relation to cultural memory making, in relation to personal memory and in terms of the relationships of remembering (Roper 2000). I want to suggest that the factors that affect the active process and creation of memories are factors that are true at any life stage.

I will explore these ideas through two examples – one from an interview conducted almost 25 years ago with an Australian First World War veteran and the second one done five or six years ago with a British woman who emigrated to Australia. Percy was 96 when I interviewed him and Joan was 66 when I interviewed her. The stage of their lives was one of the factors, just one, of the stories they told.

INTERVIEW 1 – PERCY BIRD

Setting the scene

Let me introduce Percy Bird in 1916 when he was just about to go off to the First World War. Percy grew up in a working-class family in the western suburbs of Melbourne. His father died when he was young, and his mother had a boarding house. Percy was the oldest son. When war broke out Percy was aged 26, had a job as a clerical worker for the Victorian railways and he was engaged to be married. This story does have a happy ending as Percy came back from the war, got married to his fiancée and they lived together for the next 50 years. The first extract from the interview covers issues about his enlistment. He joined the infantry in 1916, went off to war and experienced some of the worst battles of the Western Front in the winter of 1916/1917. His clerical experience probably saved his life as he was pulled out of the lines and set to work at headquarters behind the lines. Percy felt guilty about that but he got gassed *behind* the lines and was repatriated to Australia in 1917. Subsequently he had a pretty successful career in the Victorian railways (which he did not want to talk much about) and he became a semi-professional baseball player (which he did want to talk about). Most of all he wanted to talk about the window in his life that was 1916 and being a member of the Australian infantry force, the Anzacs. In the extract I try and get Percy to explain why he joined the army. He struggles with that question. In a wider context enlistment is often an emotional minefield for war veterans to remember, it may have been a difficult decision at the time, it may be a decision in retrospect they felt was a mistake, and it may well have been a decision that their society, in this case Australian society, had changing ideas about right up to the point when I interviewed Percy.

Also significant is Percy 'the narrator'. When I wrote to Percy and asked him if I could interview him, he was on the phone two hours after receiving the letter, enormously excited to be interviewed. When I turned up on his doorstep, he thrust into my hand around half a dozen pages he had written about his experiences in the battalion. The stories he had written down were pretty much the stories he wanted to tell about his experience – they were stories of concert parties behind the lines, of mates and camaraderie – they were not at all about the experience of being under fire or of going over the top or of being repatriated. He was a great storyteller and a performer – literally during the war at concert parties – and he was still a performer in interviews. The performance he wanted to give was with a set of stories that he developed over time, in this case in relation to his war experience that for him was a good story that he could live with, that made a good and positive sense of his life overall and portrayed the war as a significant and positive time of his life.

Interview extract

Can you remember where you were when the war broke out and your response to the war?

Oh yes, I was here in Melbourne, on the 4th of August 1914, and in the train from Williamstown going to Melbourne, with a number of us got in the same carriage and we saw a boat coming down the river. Hello, look at that. It was the Holzt I think the name, a German boat, trying to get out. A big artillery fired to stop them. Fired two or three shots to stop them. So they grabbed them.

What was your initial response to the war?

Oh, well, nothing particular. But I was going to join up some about February 1915 but my father was put in to hospital seriously ill. My mother said, don't do anything until we see how Dad gets on. So I enlisted somewhere early in July 1915 because they tried to operate on my father, but his heart wouldn't take it. So they said well, we'll let him have another twelve months. So he died on the 4th of March 19..., no 4th of April 1916.

Why did you want to enlist?

[laugh] I wanted to enlist like all the others, well like lots of the others I should say. Because I thought I was, I was ... should enlist being an Australian.

Analysing Percy's interview

I will examine what is happening with Percy and his remembering in this extract, and in what ways and to what extent is Percy's age as a 96-year-old a relevant feature of his remembering.

When we look at the text of the transcript we can identify three different types of narrative in that extract. The first one is a classic Percy Bird story; it is a type of anecdote that's been well honed over the years, a story that he wrote down. It is a story he wanted to tell and he would have been on the ship by the end if I had not butted in. Interestingly, I played this extract in Melbourne once to someone who understood the geography of the two rivers of Melbourne slightly better than I did. Where the railway bridge crosses the river, you cannot actually see where the Holzt was fired on from where the railway goes. So there is no way Percy actually saw the incident he describes. He may have heard it, read it in the paper or he may have been told about it. However, he has brought the event in to be his story, thereby connecting him to a significant public moment.

Then I asked the next question, what was your initial response? This brings out an extraordinary passage illustrating how when people are really working hard remembering, they are not just bringing out the story on the top but they are burrowing down trying to remember what happened. That is what happens there. This is not a story of his Dad's illness that is either comfortable or he has told very often. He is working his way; he is confused with dates and so on. He is working his way to remember something incredibly significant that happened but has not become part of his storytelling repertoire.

Finally, I asked a direct question, well why did you enlist? There is a very different narrative again. The laughter, captured on tape, is a very anxious, awkward laughter. Percy stutters and stumbles, and in the end the response is almost like the clichéd expected response 'I did it because my mates did, because I had to, because I was a member of ....' It is possible to surmise that if had he been asked in 1916 he would have said being a member of the British Empire, but in 1983 he is definitely going to say, after a short pause, being an Australian, particularly talking to a younger Australian to whom he wants to convey this generational memory of being an Australian in the First World War.

In oral history it is important to try and understand both what happened and what it means. In this case, you can explore a conflict between two different versions – a family man who has a responsibility to his family and unspoken responsibility to his fiancée and a patriotic national man who has a responsibility to his nation. Percy had a very difficult choice in 1916 and it is still a difficult choice to remember. It is not one he chooses to tell, so he struggles with remembering and would rather tell that first bit of the story. Looking at Percy's interview in terms of the factors raised before and to what extent age and later stage of life is significant, the first point is this is a 96-year-old with a remarkably robust long-term memory and yet with a very active process of the creation of meaning and remembering as part of that. The second point relates to the personal narrative creation and coherence, i.e. to what extent and in what ways is he trying to find or create a past he can live with. Clearly, over the years Percy has created a comfortable story of the war, which does not include his enlistment, because that is not a comfortable story for him.

Percy's sense of unease becomes even more acute later in the interview when we talk about life in the lines and being under fire; this is something he really does not want to talk about. What he wants to talk about is getting behind the lines and having a reasonably good time. There was one particular moment when I had gone back to interview him for the second time. The night before there had been a television programme about Australians in the First World War and during the interview he started talking about the programme and getting cross about how inaccurate it was. Suddenly there was a moment, just like opening a drawer or flood gates of remembering, and he told these terrible stories about two friends in the trench who get blown up and another one gets caught on the wire and is struggling to get off. Then he closes down again, so achieving composure. Finding a comfortable way of making sense of enlistment and the trauma of war has been very difficult and actually the story, the remembering, that he has wanted to do has been rather different

Looking at Percy's experience of life review in later life, one can see that actually even at 96 years of age Percy has not been able to look back and comfortably traverse every aspect of his life. His reaction is different to other veterans of a similar age I have interviewed. These veterans were able to return to and remember the difficult times and rethink and re-remember them, whereas Percy was not able to do that. The last paragraph of the extract illustrates how Percy is creating a story and making sense of events using cultural means and memory. He has had to live with the Anzac legend – a powerful, patriotic, national story about these Australian heroes. All through his life he's had to negotiate with those public stories in parallel with his personal narrative and remember in 1916 trying to decide whether or not to enlist and in 1983 trying to remember what type of man and what type of soldier he was.

And lastly, there is that third factor about remembering in relationships. Percy's daughter told me that he really did not talk much about the war with his family but he did talk more about it at battalion reunions. Within a year after I interviewed Percy, he went into a residential care home where he lived to be 100. The staff at the home said Percy often sat in the corner with a gathering of old women regaling them with stories of his younger life. The stories were either about him as a semi-professional baseball player or about positive aspects of his war experiences. So clearly remembering within different relationships is significant. For instance when talking to me I think there was something about the older man wanting to convey a national story to a younger generation.

From analysing these extracts of Percy's interview, I feel we one can say here that factors that influence our remembering and which are relevant to us at all stages of our lives can have a specific and distinctive significance in later life.

INTERVIEW 2 – JOAN PICKETT

Setting the scene

Joan Pickett was born in 1934 and grew up in a working-class suburb of Manchester. Joan's father was a train driver and her mother died when she was about 3 years old. Shortly after her mother died, she and her older brother Harry went to live in Blackpool for a year. Her father remarried and the children returned to Manchester to live with their father and stepmother, who worked in a local mill. Joan was a bright girl, got a scholarship to the grammar school and achieved a school leaving certificate. Then like many bright working-class girls in the late 1940s and early 1950s she was caught up in the limiting aspirations of and expectations of working-class girls with education. She had dreams of working for the BBC. The school wanted her to be a teacher but she could not think of anything worse. She sat the civil service exam and passed it, but then went along to the Manchester town hall and thought what a terrible place. Her father got her a job on the railways as a secretary and she had a very successful next ten years or so working there and then as a medical secretary in a hospital. During this time she travelled all over Europe. And then in 1960, she and her girlfriend – and this is the story extracted below – went to a cinema in Manchester and saw a newsreel about a royal visit to Australia. They remembered posters about £10 passengers to Australia and they decided on the spur of the moment to take up the offer. Joan spent the next eight years working in Australia and travelling around the country, as well as New Zealand and the Pacific having a fantastic time and was on the cusp of staying in Australia when her father died. Joan, worried about her stepmother, came back to the UK and Manchester. She got a temporary job as secretary in an electronics firm and was there for the next 23 years. She became an executive secretary in a large multinational firm and took early retirement in her late fifties. I interviewed Joan for a general project on why people go to Australia and stay or return. Joan is clearly a returnee.

Stories of motivation can be really interesting. For Percy it was why did you go to war? The question for Joan was why did you go to

Australia? To find return migrants to interview for the project[1] we issued a press release in local and regional newspapers and radio inviting return 'Ten Pound Poms' to get in touch. About 500 people replied and we then asked them to write about their experience. Approximately 252 of them wrote anything from a page to 300 pages. They sent us letters, diaries, photos and other wonderful material. Joan wrote a two-page account for the project called 'I was only kidding, memories of a ten pound pommie'. The first paragraph, which is about her story of why she went to Australia, is given below.

> It was a dark, cold midwinter evening in Manchester in January in 1960, and a work mate and I emerged from the cinema having watched news reel coverage of Princess Alexandria's tour of Australia. 'Shall we go to Australia?' I jokingly asked my friend. 'All right' she said in the same jocular manner. To while away the winter days we sent for the ten pound pommie information currently being offered by Australia House. We were soon being interviewed by a young, handsome immigration officer. We must have looked a bit guilty as he willingly informed us that they understood that many of us young things were only interested in a two-year working holiday in the sun and were fairly confident that we would be tempted to stay and settle down eventually in Australia. We agreed that if he was an example of what was waiting for us ... that we would also take the risk. Despite of and perhaps because of disbelieving work mates not to mention our own shocked families we were swept along by events and much to everyone's and our own surprise sailed through the Suez canal on the P&O liner Oronsay that same September.

Joan's story of why she went is a lovely story, beautifully crafted. There is another dimension of remembering, which is about performance and storytelling. We can be wonderful storytellers and

---

[1] 'The Forgotten Migrants: A Cultural History of Postwar British Migrants Who Returned "Home" from Australia', was the author's research project funded by the British Arts and Humanities Research Board in 2000.

also draw upon storytelling styles and genres. You can see the romantic adventure story genre that Joan has picked up and used very effectively in her account. In the interview, when I asked Joan why she went to Australia, she told a much more detailed but equally rich and vivid account of the cinema and evoked the dismal wet mid-winter evening in Manchester, in itself enough explanation of why you would want to go to Australia. Of course, in the interview, it becomes a slightly different story, not least because of the interactive nature of the dialogue. She is talking to someone who is prompting and encouraging, and she is actually re-remembering and going beyond the established initial narrative account she has provided. In the course of a long interview, other factors became significant – such as the Australian doctors she met in the hospital who encouraged her to go; the fact that she has travelled alot through her youth because of her connection with the railways and in a way going to Australia was just an extension of going around Europe. Then, in the extract below, it becomes clear there are other factors that really Joan may have sensed but not talked about before, which are significant to why she left.

I had been all over the continent because I worked on the railway cos we used to get free passes on the trains, so every year for about five or six years that I worked on the railway, we went abroad all over the continent, we went on the Simplon Orient Express to Venice, we went to Paris and we went to Austria, Italy – my father had only ever left the country once, he went to Ostend for a weekend, that was his travel. But, I don't know really, I was always curious to see places, and I think perhaps thought we were getting in a bit of a rut as you get older, and most of my friends were getting married, perhaps I felt I was being left behind in some way – I don't know what it was. But it just seemed to happen, and we just took advantage of it.

Do you think that thing getting in a rut. How important do you think that was for the decision for going?

Well, I suppose we mustn't have been completely happy in a way. But perhaps we thought – I was 26, I don't really know. I didn't try to analyse it, it's just, it just seemed to happen at the time and I just took advantage of it. But everybody was very, very surprised when I said I was leaving home. They all thought it was wonderful, but rather me than them, sort of thing. You go and tell us what it's all about. Nobody in the family had ever done anything like it and they were all rather surprised. No, we just decided, and then it's too late to turn back. Once you start doing it, it takes all your attention and you soon get over your nervousness. Looking back on it, it's all a bit of a strange episode and I don't think I would have the nerve to do it now.

The first story Joan writes and tells is a story of a dare that snowballs and becomes an adventure. It is a wonderful formed narrative of adventure travel and coming of age. That is the story she wants to tell. In the context of the interview and our relationship and the remembering work she is doing in the interview, a very different and if you like deeper level of explanation comes through. It is about being a young woman in her mid-twenties in Manchester in a very close extended family network with three aunts and dozens of cousins in the same street, who are all getting married and she is the last one left. Her brother has just got married, all of her cousins have got married and she is beginning to feel – as she says elsewhere – unusual, different, abnormal, in a rut – and what are the opportunities for a young working-class woman like her in the late 1950s. The only way she can really leave home is either to go off somewhere to train or to get married, and neither of these things are happening. Suddenly Australia emerges as an extraordinary escape route here and she cannot describe it. That is not the comfortable story she can tell. I went to Australia because I was a working-class girl, whose aspirations were limited, and I was not married, I was in a rut and I was on the shelf. In a way it is a story that between us we have got to alongside her initial story.[2] It is a very different story.

---

[2] Originals or copies of the letters, oral history interviews and other life documents have been deposited with the British Australian Migration Research Project Collection. Mass Observation Archive, University of Sussex Library.

The point here is that in the context of an interview relationship and in the context of Joan working hard with her remembering, she is able to make different and possibly deeper but certainly different and more challenging sense of what happened and why she went to Australia. It is not a particularly comfortable story for Joan to tell but it is one that actually makes another layer of sense to the story that she first told. It is a story that comes out of prompting but it is also Joan thinking about it in different ways. The influence of the women's movement and feminism that made gender and class significant factors to take into account enables Joan to place her experience and interpret it within a wider social context (Thomson, 2007). In her interview she says I have never tried to analyse, but then she does analyse what has happened to her and does so in other parts of the interview. That sort of analysis may not have been possible in the late 1950s for Joan and may still be difficult in 2000, but together it is an analysis that we worked on.

There is another extract which highlights the differences between the time of the event and the time of the telling. One of the delightful things about Joan is that she has a short journal which she started writing when she, literally, left Manchester Piccadilly on the train to London to get the ship to Australia. She kept the journal going for three weeks, then she stopped as she was having so much fun on the ship. Over the next eight years she wrote many letters, almost 300, mainly to her father, all of which we have got. The extracts below show and contrast the account of her journal which she wrote on the train within an hour of leaving Manchester Piccadilly and leaving her family, and then how she described that moment in the interview 40 years later. I will then explore the differences between these accounts and how later life and old age may be a significant factor in producing different versions of the same incident.

This is an extract from the journal:

So we were waiting for the train to move off, the minutes dragged by. Could we still turn back, no, there goes the whistle, the light is green and slowly we pull away waving furiously out of the window until the platform disappears in puffs of steam and we enter the dark night outside. We are off.

The above account was written while Joan was sitting on the train on her way to London. This is how Joan remembers that moment 40 years later:

> I got onto this night train, and I always remember there were clouds of steam. It was something like 'Brief Encounter', it was quite late at night. My father was standing there in his raincoat and his Trilby on, he kissed us and said come back if you can, but he said don't worry about us; you do what you want to do. My mother was crying of course, and we were crying [laugh] and the train pulled away and my father sort of disappeared into this cloud of smoke and I never saw him again.

While both accounts show emotion they do so for different reasons. In the first one Joan does not know she will never see her father again. Yet it is a profoundly determining factor in the second one; the event makes very different sense to her because it is the very last time she saw her father. It is the platform that disappears into the steam in the written account, whereas it is her father in the second one.

The first account is a story that is clearly looking forward, it is going into the dark night, the platform disappears – it is a story of anticipation. In the interview she talks about how emotional and nervous and how terrified she was, and she jokes how her father said that she had worn the path to the outside toilet, because she was going backwards and forwards so much in the week before she left. She was very anxious and emotional about leaving. But that is not revealed in the first account; it is really an adventure story looking forward.

An obvious difference in the narrative form is that one is a written account and one an oral account. The extract from the journal is a polished piece designed for someone else to read. Joan did have the strong sense that one day she was going to write the novel of her life, and this was a first draft, as were the many letters. She is a wonderful letter writer and writer. She is skilful in crafting a narrative with all sorts of tensions and issues as demonstrated in the journal piece. The interview extract is different in that (a) it is verbal and it is spoken to me and (b) it is relational and it is profoundly shaped by the emotionality of what she subsequently discovered. It becomes significant. It does not mean she is making things up later on but she is making a new and a different sense of that experience. It is also an account where she is actually influenced by a range of cultural narratives, such as the film 'Brief Encounter'. She has drawn upon a very private narrative in British cultural history to help her share and explain her feelings.

It is interesting to explore the differences and similarities between oral and written narratives. Both of the accounts have generic characteristics. One of them is an adventure story. The second one has a visual cinematic quality to it – not just because of the reference but because it looks like a scene, using clouds, for instance, as symbols.

There are different types of life writing shaped by similar factors including relationship, motivation, time of the telling, time of the event and generic form. In what ways does writing make different sense of storytelling from speech? An obvious way is that speaking is the most direct, immediate and interactive relationship, whereas the writing is in relationship but it is less immediate and less obviously interactive, therefore it can be considered to be more crafted and in a sense you are more in control of the material. In a spoken account in two ways perhaps you are less in control. You are less self-consciously editing as you speak, although you are self-editing, and you are also alert to the audience and shifted in mood by that dialogue over time (Perks and Thomson 2006).

For example, a laugh – as you find with any emotional point – makes you, the audience, react. There is a lot of 'non-verbal' culture taking place between the interviewer and the interviewee – interaction which otherwise you have to explain and write down. You do have to work out what a 'laugh' means in a transcript. For Joan, here, it is a powerful laugh that registers the significance of this moment, the potency of the story and the continuing resonance for her 40 years on. It turns out her relationship with her father was intensely close and significant and very positive. He was very supportive of her in Australia and constantly writing to her saying, have you found Mr Right yet? She wrote back to him about every man she met – he was almost Mr Right and then was not. Then suddenly her father is dead. She found out from a telegram and made her first phone call to England in eight years. It becomes a pivotal moment and it is also a pivotal moment – the death of her father – which shapes the rest of her life. It is the reason why she ends up back in Manchester, which she has nightmares about for the next five years and uncertainty about where she wants to be. It has other emotional baggage.

I will finish off with one last brief extract. Towards the end of the interview with Joan in 2000, I asked her about remembering – about what it was like and how it works. There are two points here – one it reminds us just how insightful our narrators can be with acute thoughts on remembering but also it reminds us that working with memory is a common currency, you can talk to anyone about them as we all have memories. Although you can bring theoretical approaches to them to make sense you can also have an informed and engaged conversation with your narrators.

Here is Joan talking about remembering:

You wrote about having a life time of memories

Yes, that's right

For you what was the significance of these memories of Australia compared to all your other memories, where does this fit?

Well they seem to be more vivid than other memories, somehow, because there was so many of them, and they were all such new experiences, and as I say if I can't sleep at night occasionally I can go back to Ocean Island and I can start walking around or driving round, you know, everything is still so vivid. Or you know I can go to Hobart and I can drive up the road to Mount Wellington – I can see it all still there. I have loads of lovely slides, of course, I must get them all collated one of these days. No it was all so vivid because it was something so completely different, the other was sort of normal and this was abnormal and so it stuck out in your memory. And, of course, if anybody ... there are things I may have done in my earlier life, before that, those weren't documented so I have probably forgotten a lot of things I did before that but this was so different and so out of the ordinary that it stays fresh all the time.

I love this passage about memory. I love the way it highlights the way significant parts of our life get remembered because they are significant at the time, because they have signposts or hooks that link them into memory. We return to them as they are meaningful to us. I love the notion she has of bringing out memories, which she certainly did. It is an active process of creation. The letters she wrote are first drafts of memories that she returns to, she brings them out again and revisits them and re-remembers and this is quite clearly something she does in relationship. In Joan's case she does not do this with grandchildren or with younger members of her family because although she did marry she did not have children and she does not have many very close nephews or nieces. However, she does have a very active life as a member of a pensioners' organisation and the University of the Third Age. She is often asked to tell the story of her time in Australia. You get a real sense of the value and significance of a particular past and a particular related story – remembered story – for Joan's sense of self and her identity in a life where she believes she did something distinctive and different. It is a past that gives value to her and that she wants to tell.

There is no doubt that life stage and old age may have a significant impact on our remembering, in terms of the distinctive nature and qualities of the relationships for remembering, or in terms of how an older individual deals with changing cultural meanings and memories in relation to their own experience, and in relation to possibly distinctive features of reviewing a life and making sense of it – both past and present – in later life. A later life stage can have a significant effect in those ways on our remembering. Yet, I think it is just as important to consider ways in which remembering in later life is shaped by social and psychological factors and narrative and relational factors that influence how we remember and tell the stories of our life at any stage, in relation to remembering influenced by cultural meanings and memories as part of an ongoing struggle to create a more or less coherent sense of ourselves and a past that we can live with.

REFERENCES

Hammerton, A.J. and Thomson, A. (2005) *Ten Pound Poms: Australia's Invisible Migrants.* Manchester: Manchester University Press.

Perks, R. and Thomson, A. (eds) (2006) *The Oral History Reader*, second edn. London: Routledge.

Roper, M. (2000) 'Re-remembering the soldier heroes: The psychic and social construction of memory in personal narratives of the Great War', *History Workshop Journal*, 50 (Autumn), 181–204.

Summerfield, P. (2004) 'Culture and composure: creating narratives of the gendered self in oral history interviews', *Cultural and Social History*, 1(1), 65–93.

Thomson, A. (1994) *Anzac Memories: Living with the Legend.* Melbourne: Oxford University Press.

Thomson, A. (2007) 'Four paradigms transformations in oral history', *Oral History Review*, 34(1), 49–70.

Thomson, A. (2010) *Moving Stories, Women's Lives.* Manchester: Manchester University Press.

4

SEX, LIVES AND VIDEOTAPE
Oral history group work and older adult education groups

GRAHAM SMITH

The concept of 'transactive' remembering is applied to a discourse analysis of video recorded group meetings with older people in an adult education setting. In doing so, this paper addresses the relationship between individual remembering and the narration of shared memories. Findings suggest that the analysis of the video recordings supports earlier insights, especially from reminiscence research. This includes the ways in which group identities are made ('re-membering'). However, as well as consensus, the analysis also identifies sharp disagreements. This 'dis-membering' reflected social differences within the groups and provides evidence of contested remembering that challenges simplistic cultural and psychological models of memory.

Oral historians writing about remembering in groups offer varied advice, but on the whole it is hard to find anyone positively in favour of group remembering as a method of data collection. Indeed most suggest that group interviews should not be attempted. I particularly like Don Ritchie's suggestion that group interviews increase the potential for trouble (Ritchie 1995: 62). This is because one of the traditions in oral history is causing trouble and that's also something I signed up to when I began working in oral history in the 1980s.

The attitudes of people other than oral historians who are working with groups are somewhat different: groups are seen to potentially provide complex dynamics and more sympathetic frameworks of understanding. This is especially so amongst the social psychologists who have written about older people and group work. And it is an area in which I was particularly interested in because I think a little more understanding of memory and remembering can be gleaned here. My interest goes back to the 1990s and the work that Joanna Bornat was involved in, along with the research of Buchanan and Middleton (1994) that was published in *Reminiscence Reviewed*. The major insight was that reminiscence is a social process. This is an important point, even if it might seem rather mundane at first sight.

Oral historians don't always observe the social processes involved in recall. We are engaged in a one-to-one interview and we don't hear how other people make memory or do remembering outside the narrow confines of the interview. As I will go on to describe, Buchanan and Middleton's arguments were also of interest to me as I had been engaged in working with groups of older people within community education in Dundee.

A more recent theoretical development that I think is relevant here is the notion of the romance of team working. Joanna Bornat has written about something similar to this in relation to working with staff or carers who are looking after older people and how the significant impact of reminiscence might not directly be about memory, but rather be about the ways in which care staff form better relationships with older people after enjoying hearing their clients remember (Gibson 1994; Smith and Bornat 1999). Allen and Hecht (2004 a,b) have made similar observations about younger people working in groups. Their idea was that people were not remembering more effectively in teams as had been supposed, but rather that team members had persuaded themselves of the efficacy of working together, because it felt good to work with others. And again this connects to the earlier work of Buchanan and Middleton (1995) in terms of how remembering with others confers identity and affirms confidence, with the interesting twist that remembering in groups might be inefficient and hamper individual recall. However, Allen and Hecht have pointed out that there is a rapid improvement in performance in groups in which the members know one another.

Before returning to this point I need to say something about the different models of memory that have developed amongst oral historians and social psychologists. I have never subscribed to the notion of collective memory; it seemed too essentialist and too fixed. It also seemed to be too easily used to provide spurious support for claims that certain collective identities existed: including national and racial identities. In other words identities that were imagined were being given substance through the 'discovery' of common memories.[1] So, for a long time I preferred to think of shared memories as social memory, then I came across the notion of transactive memory.

Transactive memory describes the process of people remembering together in relationships. Developed by Daniel M. Wegner (Wegner 1986; Wegner *et al.* 1985), amongst others, it allows for the idea that individual members of a group do not remember everything that the group as a whole remembers. In our small social sets (family, colleagues, friends) we cooperate in remembering, and through communicating we can share many more memories as a group than any one individual could ever remember. I became acutely aware of this when after my father's death my mother claimed that she had forgotten the drive between her home and the supermarket. Together we figured out that this was something my father had known – he had for many years been responsible for that drive – and with his death my mother had suffered transactive memory loss.

Transactive memory or remembering is a useful concept because it might move us on from modernist notions of the collective, including work inspired by the often cited, seldom read, Halbwachs (1992) (on memory) or Jung (1971) (on the unconscious). It might also be useful, because it has the potential of explaining how individual memories and shared memories are linked together. But how useful is it in understanding how older people remember in different situations?

In the 1980s I was part of a community group that recorded the recollections of 100 Dundonians. And then a decade later I was employed by the local council to establish making history groups with older people who were living in sheltered housing complexes in the city. Much more recently I began to think about the difference between memories collected in the groups and those collected on a one-to-one basis.

The making history groups were sponsored by the Regional Council's Community Education division. My remit was to engage

---

[1] For a longer exploration of this argument see Smith and Jackson 1999.

with these groups in ways that would encourage members to recall the past *and* open a dialogue with the local authority's service providers. One of the things we did was to invite officials along from the housing department and other council employees who were ostensibly my colleagues. The older people questioned a range of council managers, often in a critical manner, about why front doors were not fixed, why bins remained un-emptied, why benches weren't repaired and a whole host of other issues. It was an interesting experiment and it seemed a valuable way of raising political activity amongst older people. But the bit I want to say more about is how we prepared for these meetings by discussing the past.

In doing so, I want to talk about one group in particular. The group involved twenty women and one man. The gender imbalance was somewhat typical of the other groups; and this is not simply a matter of survival rates, but that women tended to be more attracted to reminiscence activities than men. The average age was around 77 years. We ran weekly meetings from 1990 to 1997, with around forty meetings held each year. The meetings were video recorded between 1992 and 1995. The recordings were simply intended for group members to have a look at, although copyright and ethical clearances were adhered to. Together we produced a booklet called 'Work or Want' that was published by Community Education.

My relationship with the group changed over time.[2] I started off as a facilitator and ended up as a member. If you work long enough on an oral history project you become a repository of other people's memories, even memories from before you were born, which is the weirder side of transactive remembering: we don't need to directly experience an event to be able to report on that event as if it were remembered.

Dundee is one of those towns in Britain that people talk about being big villages. There are various reasons for that – sometimes it has to do with size – but often it is the industrial or employment base of a place. As a result of a single industry dominating a local economy people end up having commonality. There are a lot of shared

---

[2] See Smith 2007 for more details on the power relations within the group and a longer discussion of transactive memory.

experiences, even if people haven't met each other, thus the sense of village. Most older Dundonians had worked in the city's jute textile industry or in industries allied to jute. It was an industry, even in the late nineteenth century, that had employed large numbers of married women and even up to the interwar years employment patterns had meant that the number of adult women continued to outnumber men. The women had a history of asserting themselves in ways that might not have been the case elsewhere in Scotland. Therefore, it would be completely wrong of me to give the impression that I was running these groups and that this was some sort of study.

So the first approach we agreed to take, after much discussion, was to ask people to take a turn in telling a story about their life in some detail on a topic. The second one we tried was a free for all collaboration. The first thing I learnt about working with the group is that older people don't play by the rules. My first example that is taken from the video recordings shows how taking a turn means different things to different people.

The following discussion makes reference to the variety of hot food outlets that were important in a city where large numbers of married women were in paid employment. But it begins with Jo, whose turn it is, talking about football.

> *Jo:* You couldnae see the Hilltoon [a long road in Dundee] for the men coming out of the [football] match. There was no nonsense. Is that right Liz?
> *Liz:* Not like now.
> *Nellie H:* Do you mind the shop that had the fruit outside on display?
> *Jo:* Then there was Edmonds the cook shop across the road that sold the tripe and a'thing. When you were working you used to tak a jug of soup or a plate of stovies for dinner. Nae bother at a'. You mind o' that Mary?
> *Mary:* Aye.
> *Jo:* And when the men came from the match ... you'd go to see if your father had any money left. And if he had any money left he'd took us over to Edmonds for a tripe supper...

Liz: Did that shop [Edmonds] hae a huge teapot in the windae?

Jo: Naw.

Liz: I wisnae fae the Hilltoon

Nellie H: Then there was Lady Mary's Fair. That was when things were coming up a bit you know if you had the money. We had the buster stalls; that was peas and chips, marvellous. The wife Déjeuner, she belonged the Overgate [area of the city] and owned buster stalls.

Mary: Déjeuner – she was German?

Evelyn: No French.

Liz: A big family.

Jo: Aye they had the buster stalls.

Liz: That was pea and chips.

Jo: Marvellous.

Liz: Got them straight off the brazier – an early version of the barbecue.

Jo is supposed to be the focus of the group's remembering and she is telling her story, but in doing so she shifts attention to other members of the group, mainly the oldest women, allowing for the opportunity of free-for-all discussion, before she speaks again. This is partly to be inclusive and may even be an attempt to avoid being seen as dominating the conversation, but more significantly she is ensuring that she can tell her story with the support of other group members. Jo invites others to show that they understand her story. The whole process results in promoting group solidarity, but it also involves the creation of transactive memories of a common past. What we see is a rhythm of remembering, a moving across and between the members. Liz plays the part of connecting the past and present. Right away she says 'not like now'. Jo asks Mary to confirm the memories about food before she neatly connects back to the men coming out of the football ground. And then the discussion moves back to food and on to belonging. But above all else is the use of 'you' – a pattern repeated in all of the recorded sessions – it is an inclusive 'you' that illustrates how transactive remembering, which feels good as an activity, is continuously sought by members of the group.

This extract is a very short one compared to the total recording of fourteen hours, and even shorter compared to three-hour meetings held on forty Friday afternoons each year for seven years. But the extract exemplifies what it was like for most of the time. The majority of the talk was similar to this example. At the time I was less than happy about the way the women were remembering. I wanted to be an oral historian. I wanted to be interviewing people. I wanted to be leading these groups, but I wasn't going to get much of a chance. Most of the time the group directed itself, expanding on topics at will. It often came back to connecting the past to the present. They often spoke about places within the town and belonging and identity. It was often nostalgic. And it was about creating shared memory. Participants corrected one another on detail, while, for most of the time, agreeing on meaning, which seems to be another feature of transactive memory.

Within the recordings there is also evidence of the boundaries of transactive remembering; when memories cannot be shared in this way. These examples are few and far between, but are worth looking at in more detail, because they offer a further insight into the nature of transactive remembering.

The first way that transactive remembering was bounded was when important experiences were not shared and meaning was hidden from the participants of history. One example is the ways household arrangements and family structures shaped childhoods. According to both Census returns and surviving rent book records between 1870 and 1940 a third of all households were headed by women in Dundee. On re-examining the 100 individual interviews that had been audio recorded in the 1980s, the existence of such large numbers of female headed households was not reflected in the recollections to the extent that might have been expected. It was in one of the subsequent turn-taking group sessions that light was thrown on the issue. Here Nellie H is telling her story recalling living as a child with her mother and grandmother.

Nellie H: I mean I didnae ken [know] no better, because there was never a man in the house ... My granny aye had a house of her own until she went blind. Then we took her to bide with us in Annfield.

Graham: Some folk would have said you would have missed a father?

Nellie H: No I didnae minda [remember] missing a father. I used to wonder how other folk had a dad, or a dai, as they cried them in they days ... but never thought anything of it. Of course I was aye with my mother, my mother took us a'place with her, up till I was about maybe thirteen or fourteen. She used to take us a'place with her.

This is one of the more unusual moments in the recordings in that I'm making an intervention. Nellie H seems somewhat puzzled about why I'm even asking the question about missing a father. In the free-for-all discussion that followed it emerged that around a quarter of the group's members were brought up in a household without a father being present. Frances B then takes up the account. She begins by speaking somewhat tangentially about getting a job and leaving home in 1928 aged 14 years. She left she said 'to live with this woman'. She is asked whether this was a landlady that she was living with.

Frances: No. She just wanted somebody to mind her bairn to let her out to work and I said I would do it. And that's how I come with her.

Graham: How did you know her?

Frances: I don't ken [know] now, I just got in with her. We used to all congregate on the plett [a tenement landing] and a'body [pause] you kent [knew] each other. And she said she wanted to go out to work and she'd nobody to mind her bairn.

Graham: Did you have to pay board?

Frances: Aye. Aye. Right on the bell. She didnae leave me an awful lot, but I liked where I lived. I didn't get on with my old man [father].

Graham: Did you pay less to her than you would to your mother?

Frances: Oh no, I'd give my mother my pay. ... I wouldnae give her it.

50

... Sometimes she'd pick a fight.

The differences in recalled childhood experiences became significant to group members as they began to contrast what it was like to grow up in a home with a father present and one in which a father was absent. The group concluded that having a father at home was not always a good thing. In doing so there was also the realisation that some memories could not be shared through the whole group. Experiences of living in something called 'female headed households' was not shared as a common experience and could not become a transactive memory.

Finally, I want to look at conflicts and disagreements and their relationship to transactive memory. One afternoon the group had drifted into a free-for-all discussion of sex, loneliness and fear in the Second World War. The discussion had been initiated by me asking if they would like to see the Age Exchange package, 'What did you do in the war?' And before discussion had even started one of the younger members said 'I know what she did in the war', pointing to her friend, 'Every bloody serviceman who visited Dundee.' This was not an auspicious start for the meeting and the free-for-all that followed became heated. At first the older women remain silent, while the younger women, along with Willie (the only man participating) transact memory.

> *Ruby:* There was plenty men. Plenty forces. There were sailors, soldiers, airmen. Foreigners, not just British.
> *Christine:* Polish, French, Yanks.
> *Ruby:* You might as well have fun.
> *Unidentified:* You didn't want to die wondering
> *Ruby:* And anybody who says they didn't [pause] I think they were a bit of a liar. You might die the morn.

The exchange continues between Willie, Ruby and Christine. They talk about loneliness, fear excitement, casual sex, prostitution and men serving overseas. But on this occasion the growth of the transactive memory is challenged.

> *Agnes [outraged]:* My man was away six years and I never done a thing.

Willie: Aye, but you're an angel.

[Raised voices]

Agnes: And he [husband] was away six years.

Willie: And he was never with a woman?

Agnes: Well maybe he did, but I never went with a man. I can vouch my life on that.

Uproar follows with the women dividing their support between Agnes and Willie.

I thought this is going to be the end of the group. We had had a happy time of memories of food, family and football matches, and all sorts of other things. I felt pretty miserable and was surprised on returning the following Friday to find that the group had found a resolution by creating two transactive memories. They had decided that the difference was about age. Those who had been in their late teens or early twenties during the war had gone on to talk about the freedom they had experienced. Ruby and Christine, for example, had both served in London in the Hyde Park anti-aircraft battery and Willie had left home to join the navy. Meanwhile Agnes and the older women had discussed the deprivations and isolation of wives and mothers who had been often stuck in a textile job while trying to run a home. Worries about husbands serving in the forces and shortages of essentials peppered the memories of the oldest women. By the time I got back to the group they had worked it out. The members of the group had tacitly agreed that there were limits to the memories they could agree upon as being shared by all.

The final story presented here is Ruby's. She is a skilful storyteller. She begins by speaking about serving on the anti-aircraft battery. The role of women in anti-aircraft batteries was quite common. This was probably the closest women in Britain got to being combatants in the Second World War and Winston Churchill agonised over whether they should be allowed to fire the guns. It was clear that as Ruby told the story, the other women admired the role she and other battery members had played. This was even more significant, because she was able to say she had met Churchill, whose daughter had also served at Hyde Park.

The Churchill connection has a particular resonance for Dundonians. The political history of Dundee in the period between the world wars was one of growing support for temperance and prohibition at the expense of the sitting Member of Parliament, Winston Churchill. In the 1922 election Churchill lost his 'seat of convenience' to the only prohibitionist, Edwin Scrymgeour, to be elected to a British Parliament by a constituency that was said to have had more pubs per square mile than any other in the country. The Scottish Prohibition Party had a great deal of success in attracting a large number of working class women into its ranks and the vote of the newly enfranchised working class women was thought to be especially important in Churchill's defeat. The Scottish Prohibition Party was also to the left of the Labour Party; calling, for example, for the nationalisation of the jute industry.

In the interviews collected in the 1980s the dislike of Churchill is evident in many of the individual testimonies. A number of interviewees claim to have witnessed Churchill's last hours in the city, when it is claimed that he and his wife were physically driven out. The image of the pearls being snatched from the neck of Clementine Churchill by the women of Dundee is a recurring symbolic image in these stories. So the following story that Ruby had begun by tapping into the anti-Churchill mythology and the public solidarity that anti-Churchillian sentiment generates, but then she moves from the public political (Churchill) to the politically private (life with her husband).

> *Ruby:* We used to think your man was the gaffer [foreman] and what he said went. A lot of people will say, 'Oh I had a marvellous life. I had a great life.' But no-body can say that, because we all have a skeleton of some kind in the cupboard. There were a lot of happy times. But if they said they had a braw [fine] man or a braw wife they are telling a lot of lees [lies].
>
> *Indistinct interruption by Elizabeth P.*
>
> *Ruby:* If there is one perfect marriage I have to bloody hear it yet.
>
> *Elizabeth P:* Well I think my daughter has a perfect marriage.

Ruby: Aye well you dinnae ken [know] that. [Very aggressively] No. No. You *might* be able to say *you* had a perfect marriage. You cannae say *he* [pointing to Willie] had a perfect marriage or your daughter or granddaughter. You don't live with them. You have to live with a person before you can say it's great. A lot of people had good men, but it doesn't make a perfect marriage.

Elizabeth P: Well what makes a perfect marriage?

Ruby: I don't think there is such a thing.

Elizabeth P: [Aghast] Oh no.

Ruby: There's a lot of people who have a happy marriage – a long happy marriage.

Nelllie H: They say true love never runs smooth.

Ruby: That's true. My man could be sitting in a crowd like this. And everybody would be happy. And then he'd say [she whispers] 'You fucking mind your own business.' He was controlling me. ... But who would take in a woman with two kids. I stuck with him for 39 years. I done my duty.

Elizabeth P: It would have been worse to have been ignored.

Graham: It's sad.

Ruby: But you get over it. There's nothing worse than a jealous man [pause] or a jealous woman.

This is a skilful bit of storytelling that begins tapping into the social and transactive memories of Churchill and then goes on to talk about experiences specific to her own life, but in such a way that opens up the possibility for others with similar experiences to join her story. In doing so she first states her membership of the group by doing transactive remembering (women/Churchill/war work), and that then provides the licence for her to tell of her difficult marriage and even more significantly she gains the opportunity for herself to tell a story that is too often silenced by those who would claim that marriages should be remembered as positive. Ruby moves from re-membering to dis-membering.

In conclusion, working in groups made me rethink about what was going on in remembering. It made me realise that there were processes between individual and social memory that require more attention. One of these processes – transactive remembering – suggests that we share memory at a level beyond individually recalled direct experiences. While there are rhythms of remembering when people are doing transactive memory, we should be aware that such remembering may be covering significant differences within groups, including generational differences of experience. We should also realise that attributing meaning or not being able to attribute meaning to memories will shape the transaction of memories. And finally, Ruby teaches us that we should always be conscious of the stories that transactive remembering can potentially silence if we are not strong enough.

REFERENCES

Allen, N.J. and Hecht, T.D. (2004a) 'The "romance of teams": Toward an understanding of its psychological underpinnings and implications', *Journal of Occupational and Organizational Psychology*, 77(4), 439–461.

Allen, N.J. and Hecht, T.D. (2004b) 'Further thoughts on the romance of teams: A reaction to the commentaries', *Journal of Occupational and Organizational Psychology*, 77(4), 485–491.

Buchannan, K. and Middleton, D. (1994), 'Reminiscence reviewed: A discourse analytic perspective', in J. Bornat (ed.) *Reminiscence Reviewed: Achievements, Evaluations, Perspectives*. Buckingham: Open University Press, pp. 61–73.

Buchannan, K. and Middleton, D. (1995) 'Voices of experience: Talk, identity and membership in reminiscence groups', *Ageing & Society*, 15(4), 457–491.

Gibson, F. (1994) 'What can reminiscence contribute to people with dementia?', in J. Bornat (ed.) *Reminiscence Reviewed: Perspectives, Evaluations, Achievements*. Buckingham: Open University Press.

Halbwachs, M. (1992) *On Collective Memory*. Chicago: The University of Chicago Press.

Jung, C.G. (1971) *Psychological Types*. Princeton: Princeton University Press.

Ritchie, D. (1995) *Doing Oral History*. New York: Twayne Publishers.

Smith, G. (2007) 'Beyond individual/collective memory: Women's transactive memories of food, family and conflict', *Oral History*, 35(2), 77–90.

Smith, G. and Bornat, J. (1999) 'Oral history, biography, life history: Broadening the evidence', *British Journal of General Practice*, 49, 770-771.

Smith, G. and Jackson, P. (1999) 'Narrating the nation: The "imagined community" of Ukrainians in Bradford', *Journal of Historical Geography,* 25(3), 367–387.

Wegner, D.M. (1986) 'Transactive memory: A contemporary analysis of the group mind', in B. Mullen and G.R. Goethals (eds), *Theories of Group Behavior*. New York: Springer-Verlag, pp. 185–208.

Wegner, D.M., Giuliano, T. and Hertel, P. (1985) 'Cognitive interdependence in close relationships', in W.J. Ickes (ed.) *Compatible and Incompatible Relationships*. New York: Springer-Verlag, pp. 253–276.

5

EXPERIENCE SHARED AND VALUED
Creative development of personal
and community memory

PAM SCHWEITZER

For 25 years I have been recording the memories of older Londoners, both in groups and individually. These have not been life story interviews, such as might be conducted in a conventional oral history context. The interviews have been undertaken in connection with many different arts-based reminiscence projects, and have focused on particular events, periods and issues. The recorded and transcribed interviews have formed the basis of many creative projects including pieces of verbatim theatre, books of edited stories and photos, 2- and 3-dimensional exhibitions and interactive installations.[1]

BACKGROUND

The broader context for this work in the 1970s and early 1980s was a growing recognition of the value to health and wellbeing of older people in the sharing of memories with others of the same generation.[2] In parallel there was an increasing acknowledgement of the potential benefits to a community's health and wellbeing from sharing life experience across the generation divide. Finally, the arts and museums worlds were slowly recognising the value of recording memories which could form the basis for shows and exhibitions.

My own professional background is in theatre and education. In my twenties and thirties I had taught creative drama and improvisation in schools, colleges and at university level. Parallel with this direct drama work, I developed a particular interest in Theatre in Education (TIE), a powerful movement in the late 1960s

---

[1] See end of article for edited list of publications.
[2] The *Recall* pack originated by Mick Kemp and developed at Help the Aged Education Department was particularly effective in popularising the group reminiscence approach.

and throughout the 1970s, in which professional actors used extended role play and performance over a whole day to capture the imagination and emotional intelligence of school children of all ages and to help them to engage with important historical, current and inter-personal issues normally considered beyond their understanding (Schweitzer 1975). Children who were apparently apathetic or obstructive in conventional classroom situations were able to relate to the dramatic situations the TIE groups presented, and were able to 'shine' for a day in ways which affected positively their teachers' subsequent perception of them and their capacities. Teachers were able to draw on the learning from these TIE productions for several weeks, and the outside stimulus effect was surprisingly powerful.

I now see that there was a distinct connection between my involvement with TIE work and the approach to reminiscence theatre I went on to develop and will describe next. There was in both theatre forms a special relationship established between actors and audience, the performers remaining in close physical proximity to the audience, and the performers inter-acting with the audience during and after the performance. In both forms, the performers called on and deferred to the experience and wisdom of the audience, speaking to them directly from the stage as much as to one another. Finally, in both theatre forms there was the potential for transformation, both in the way audience members perceived themselves and in the way they were perceived by those in charge of them (their teachers) or those caring for them (their care staff).

FIRST ENCOUNTERS WITH REMINISCENCE

In 1982, I started working for Task Force (later known as Pensioners Link, a radical voluntary sector group working with pensioners) as an education officer and soon encountered a reminiscence group in action at Minnie Bennett Sheltered Housing Unit in Greenwich. I was excited by the power of the stories emerging, immediately seeing their dramatic potential and the educational value they would afford for younger generations. I decided to create a specialist theatre company dedicated to this idea. I was also struck by the enlivening effect of the group-remembering process on participants in their late eighties to nineties and their evident relish for the activity as an occasion for personal reflection and social interaction. Never having worked with older people before, what surprised me most was the idea that they appeared to have all their past selves inside them, and that they could access these through shared reminiscence, and then benefit from the rejuvenating effect of joint retrospection. Far from being an unhealthy indulgence, as was generally thought even by some older people themselves at the time, it was clearly a tonic, as witnessed by shining faces, laughter and unwonted fluency and articulacy. The group I visited had had some professional input from Task Force and had produced their own little book of memories, illustrated with their own photographs. It had made a great difference to how they now saw themselves: as sources of interesting important experience, which was worth preserving and transmitting.

The older people at Minnie Bennett House were delighted at the prospect of undertaking some joint work with young people who wanted to make plays from their memories. I designed a series of small-scale inter-generational pilot projects to explore the possibilities further. The older people gave group and private interviews, watched rehearsals and attended performances. The whole process was energising for both groups and, on the whole, constructive, though some of the younger people did not enjoy being 'corrected' by their elders. The dilemma of accuracy versus creativity needed to be thought about and discussed with all parties. It was also felt to be rather a shame that the young people could only do one or two performances because of their school schedules, though there was clearly a great deal more potential for further showings for other older people in other venues.

REMINISCENCE THEATRE: AN EMERGING ARTFORM

All this was invaluable background experience when, in 1983, I set up Age Exchange, a professional theatre company whose work would be based entirely on the material supplied by the older people interviewed, both in reminiscence groups and individually. The actors, mostly aged between 25–45, would rehearse and perform under Equity touring contracts and the productions created from the elders' memories could have a much wider airing, with one or two performances a day, each in a different venue, for 12 weeks or longer, reaching thousands of people, especially older people who normally had no access to professional theatre.

Of course, this was a very expensive undertaking, but the Greater London Council (GLC) was offering support at the time to cultural projects favouring women, ethnic minorities and elders, and my proposal fitted their criteria. The GLC funded Age Exchange from 1983 until its own demise in 1986–7, and with GLC support, interviewers, writers and actors were taken on for specific reminiscence theatre projects. There was a small basic staff of director, administrator and stage and company manager to maintain the company between productions and to develop new work. The Manpower Services Commission, a major unemployment scheme of the time, enabled us to take on young people to transcribe interviews onto computer (a very new idea at the time, and one which enabled us to use a great deal of verbatim text in the eventual theatre scripts) and to involve them in all aspects of the theatre production process.

The company worked with different writers and they all had their own views of the way to use the transcribed interview material. Some loved the precision of using verbatim text, relishing the language chosen by the story-teller and how it reflected the age of the teller and specific time-related references.[3] A few found that verbatim was more of a straight-jacket and wanted to interpret the interview material more loosely. This gave different productions their own stamp, but all had a feeling of authenticity to the intended audience, because most of them had had a very direct input from the older people concerned, at interview stage or during rehearsals and discussions with the performers and director.

The company went on to create between three and five professional shows each year, all based on the reminiscences of older Londoners of key areas of their lived experience. These included

---

[3] I owe a debt of gratitude here to Chrys Salt who introduced me to this form and also to Joyce Holliday, who produced some of Age Exchange's strongest verbatim scripts, having honed this approach through her work with Peter Cheeseman at the Victoria Theatre, Stoke.

projects focusing on memories of starting work ('My First Job'), unemployment ('The Fifty Years Ago Show'), health ('Can We Afford the Doctor?'), housing ('Just Like the Country'), war ('What Did You Do in the War, Mum?'), love ('The Time of Our Lives'), retirement ('Many Happy Retirements') and the memories of many immigrant communities ('A Place To Stay' and 'Routes'). With additional support from charitable trusts, local authorities, arts bodies and older people's organisations, we were able to tour the productions across the country, and thence to many European countries, all performances free of charge to older people. This volume of professional reminiscence theatre work continued unabated till the end of 2004, with funding from a very wide range of sources taking over when the GLC was wound up.

REMINICENCE CENTRE: A SHOW-CASE FOR REMINISCENCE ARTS

Parallel with the development of the theatre company was the creation of the first Reminiscence Centre in Blackheath, south-east London, with a programme of changing exhibitions, meeting groups, performances and reminiscence-related activities. Three or four exhibitions were created each year, often following similar themes to the touring theatre productions, and users of the Reminiscence Centre contributed their memories and memorabilia to professionally designed interactive exhibitions.

Because each display was on a different theme, new contributors or 'sources' were drawn in and often these people became very involved in the activities of the centre and the development of the shows and exhibitions. For example, if the subject was women's war work, we relied on adverts in the local paper to invite local elders who wanted to contribute to get in touch. We would then visit and record them, or arrange for them to meet and talk to others with related memories at the Reminiscence Centre. In this way, the collection of memories kept the Centre alive and dynamic, with new projects every few months, unlike more elaborate museum-based exhibitions which tend to stay in situ over very long periods and rely on different visitors coming through all the time. In the case of the

Reminiscence Centre exhibitions, the recorded memories were edited and displayed (including the names of the original speakers) alongside artefacts, but also supported by full-scale murals, built environments and opportunities for interaction. This made a visually stimulating for the memories and enabled visitors of different ages and cultures to engage with the subject matter and offer their own contributions.

Using theatre-designers rather than museum exhibition designers gave a completely different feel to the exhibitions, more informal, more hand-painted, in many ways more inclusive. When a new exhibition was in preparation, older people would drop by to look at the model for the finished display, to see how things were progressing and often to lend additional objects and images and to give practical help.

Everything in the finished exhibition could be handled, which made a great difference to people's capacity to remember, and we found that the Reminiscence Centre became a real target for homes and hospitals looking for ways to stimulate their elders. Small groups would visit the exhibitions, and individuals would linger by particular objects for several minutes, hold them and then, perhaps for the first time in a long while, be moved to tell a personal memory stimulated by the object in its rich context of related reminiscence items, murals and displays. Many of the exhibitions featured ethnic minority memories and promoted the mixing and mutual appreciation of groups of elders who would normally have little interaction. These minority-based exhibitions were particularly appreciated by local schools, giving a strong inter-generational and inter-cultural flavour to the Reminiscence Centre.

GATHERING REMINISCENCES FOR THEATRE PRODUCTIONS

The interviews in connection with theatre productions and exhibitions were recorded for immediate use, popular consumption, and the widest possible distribution rather than for scholarly purposes, archival storage or for posterity. But that is not to say there was no legacy element. Recognising that theatre is an essentially evanescent form and that the stories collected in connection with each project would hold tremendous interest both now and in the future, we decided early on that every show based on memories would have a book to go with it. In this way, we could keep the shows alive in the audiences' minds, stimulate further their own memories and enable care staff working with older people to build on the performance through subsequent reminiscence sessions in their venues.

A further incentive in undertaking this publishing task was that almost all the people interviewed had left school at 14 years of age and were less happy exploring their past lives in writing than in conversation. They were highly unlikely to commit their vivid memories to paper, so these sound recordings were an invaluable record of the lived experience of these so-called 'ordinary people'. By gaining financial subsidy for the books we could go for long print-runs of 3–4,000 to keep unit costs low, and sell large numbers of them at half price (mostly £1 or £2) to pensioners at every show. This populist approach to publishing older people's memories and photos in edited form encouraged many groups across the UK in clubs and care establishments to produce home-grown collections of older people's stories.[4]

GROUP AND INDIVIDUAL MEMORIES

For every project there were group reminiscence sessions and individual interviews. In many cases the group sessions led naturally into one-to-one recordings as people with particularly rich memories realised they had much more they could tell than could be easily fitted into a group session, or as the interviewers recognised particular individuals with strong stories to tell and a will to tell them.

A group reminiscence session would normally be run by the director, the actors, the writers or the researchers in lounges or day rooms or community centres where older people congregated. Objects,

---

[4] The Community Publishing movement of the 1970s and 1980s (including Centreprise and Peckham Book Place) was flourishing at this time and influenced our policy.

images and music related to the topic would be available for people to listen to, handle and talk about to break the ice and to stimulate memory. Sessions might begin quite informally exploring these collections of objects while music was played in the background and the whole group gathered.

The person leading the session would introduce the project, explaining its intended theatre outcome, outlining the proposed theme of the play and some of the topics it might explore, and inviting responses. The discussions which followed were wide-ranging and socially inclusive. The session leaders always tried to ensure that the 'air-time' was shared and that encouraged people to join in, even with very short contributions. People were welcome just to listen to other people's stories if that was what they preferred, and to enjoy joining in some of the songs remembered.

RECORDING INTERVIEWS

Although these sessions had a practical purpose and were very informal in nature, they were always tape-recorded. We were not at the time thinking of storing or archiving these recordings in a sound form, and we did not intend to use any recording directly in the shows. We just wanted to transcribe exactly what was said and use the paper versions in our scripting, exhibitions and books. Passing a portable tape-recorder round a group often meant that volume levels were variable (according to how loud or quiet were the speakers' voices) and there was often background noise from neighbouring rooms, the rattle of tea-cups or even the lounge canary! Amazingly, many of the recordings are still audible 20 years later, but there are all sorts of technical difficulties in retrospectively converting the material we collected into archiveable digitised sound files. However, the interviews collected over more than 20 years concerning so many aspects of twentieth century life as remembered by older people do constitute a unique collection which will need to be stored safely.

DEVELOPING A SENSE OF COMMUNITY
THROUGH REMINISCENCE

Most of the participants found the reminiscence sessions held in connection with our projects to be enjoyable and rewarding social occasions. They would be hearing stories from one another which they had not heard before, which were interesting in themselves and which often triggered long-forgotten memories of their own. They could establish common bonds with other people participating in the group and pursue these links both within the session and after it. In this way, the reminiscence activity provided new opportunities for people to make new contacts and friendships. We realised how important this element was as we moved from one sheltered housing unit or home to another setting up reminiscence sessions; people often knew little of one another's past lives, although they were sharing a living space. In fact many were lonely, though surrounded by people, since there were not many opportunities to get to know about one another and discover common bonds.

Indeed, people sharing memories in these group sessions often developed a sense of community through discovering that their histories had much in common; that they had all lived through the same social, political, economic and cultural changes and reacted to them in their individual ways. There was often a sense of 'we' and 'us', which developed through sharing memories, and also a sense that they had been participants in history and part of the wider changing social fabric they were evoking and recalling. A participant in a reminiscence session set up for one of our theatre projects wrote to us as follows:

> It was a lovely experience to meet people of the same age and to re-experience memories. As you listen to other people's stories, more and more comes back to you, even memories which had not been brought to light for many years. It was a true joy to hear about other people's memories and to tell about and live through again your own.

For those whose experience had been different from the majority, because of cultural or ethnic background, a reminiscence session like this could be an opportunity to become known and appreciated, especially where the facilitator welcomed and valued the difference and singularity of the individual experience. For the purpose of play-making, such difference in background and perception was essential, so that the eventual piece could reflect a range of contrasting experience, rather than reproducing only the dominant view.

HEARING AND BEING HEARD

Many people sharing memories in these groups were unused to speaking (and hearing themselves speak) in any sort of public forum and were surprised and delighted by the responses they evinced. At best, these sessions left people with a sense that they were valued members of an interesting group, that they had been part of a desirable social event and that they had made a real contribution to the forthcoming show with its accompanying book.

Where individual interviews were conducted, still with reference to the forthcoming production, people had more opportunity to think back on particular personal episodes and how they had reacted to changing circumstances and broader social upheavals. Encouraged by questions from the interviewer concerning details of time, place, others involved and associated feelings, older people were often able to re-enter the past and recapture it with unprecedented clarity. Even though these were not 12-hour life story interviews, but usually only an hour long and focusing on a limited subject area, the older people said that they found the experience of the interview rewarding and revealing. Many people said they had carried on remembering for a long time after the interview itself had ended.

THE TRANSITION FROM RECORDING TO END-PRODUCT: AN INCLUSIVE PROCESS

The conversion from original recording to end-product was also a participatory, socially inclusive process, in which older people were invited to attend rehearsals, support particular actors and offer input and ideas to the team concerning the playing out of their own stories; in effect, they were directing their own scenes. Observing the actors performing parts of their lives invariably offered a tremendous jolt to their memory, so that hitherto forgotten details came to mind and could be fed into the evolving script.

This direct involvement gave the older people a stronger sense of ownership of the production, with many inviting family and friends to see 'my show'.

It also made a great difference to the actors having the originators of their scenes present in rehearsal. Some were wary of having anyone in rehearsal and felt no-one should see work in progress, but rather wait for the finished product. This sometimes led to a certain tension as there was not always quite enough rehearsal time anyway, especially with complicated instrumental parts and harmonies to learn. However, for most actors, it gave them a sense that they were carrying a real person's experience, which usually increased their commitment to the role and enabled them to see this as a special kind of performance undertaking. It was also of practical value since the older people could explain how a job was done (for example lifting a hundredweight bag of sugar with a docker's hook or threshing corn on a steam thresher in the Land Army) or how a song might have been delivered, with actions remembered by the older people from childhood. For example, in 1985 Iris Gange gave us a poem she had written in 1941 about being a telephone switchboard operator in the WAAF. When we set this to music in the acapella style of the Andrews Sisters, very popular at that time, Iris came to rehearsal, was delighted with the song and set about choreographing the cast's movements so that what they were doing would make sense to viewers, would stir memories and, above all, ensure absolute authenticity in the scene performance. In many cases strong bonds developed between performers and the people they were playing, and the older people remembered with great fondness the actors who had presented their 'younger selves' and their own direct experience of working on the play.

PUBLISHING THE MEMORIES COLLECTED
FOR THE SHOWS

The books of stories, which accompanied the shows, were edited around the key themes covered, but the specific style and word choice of the original speakers was preserved.[5] The 'sources' were always shown their edited pieces to make sure they were happy with them. This was not always straightforward, as people were often surprised when they saw what they had said on tape in written form, so we allowed people to remove or edit passages if they were uncomfortable with the original telling. The books were illustrated with the carefully preserved photographs supplied by the interviewees and local collections, which enabled them to trigger more memories by association and helped the reader to enter into the spirit of the period or topic described. Given that many of the consumers of the shows and the books were younger people or people from a different social or cultural background, the images gave a visual context to the memories and made the past experience of the older people more accessible to them. Some of these thematic illustrated reminiscence books were reprinted several times, running into 5,000 or more copies, especially 'What Did You Do in the War, Mum?', 'Can We Afford The Doctor?' and many were used as reminiscence stimulus in homes, hospitals and community groups long after the shows had finished touring. Care staff used the books as a stimulus for their increasingly common reminiscence activities and schools used them to study the recent past, often contacting the theatre company with a view to inviting older contributors into the classroom to work with their children.

Knowing that their stories would be performed in the present, displayed in an exhibition and preserved in print for the future gave the older contributors a greater sense of investment in these reminiscence-based projects. They were intrigued by the prospect of being dramatised and enthusiastic about the idea of their recorded

---

[5] 'On the River' (about work in the London Docks) and 'Goodnight Children Everywhere' (about wartime evacuation of London children to the countryside) were particularly popular titles, but altogether about 30 books were published by Age Exchange in these years and most are still extant.

memories outliving them in printed form. It was always noticeable that, when a volunteer had been on duty welcoming people to the Reminiscence Centre, the books would fall open at 'their page'.

THE RELATIONSHIP OF THE 'SOURCES' TO REMINISCENCE ARTS

It was important to make clear to the interviewees the purpose of the recording sessions. We were not asking people to give a life-story interview, but were concentrating on what they wanted to tell us about a particular aspect of their lives, perhaps their experience of moving to one of the new LCC (London County Council) housing estates, or their stories about going hop-picking every autumn in Kent, or their experience of coping with unemployment in the 1920s and 1930s. Of course, people did stray well outside the given topic, but they were always clear that we had a very direct purpose in recording them and that they were helping us in our quest. We were gathering stories together around the chosen theme in order to provide material for a scripted play, often with a related exhibition and almost always with an accompanying book.

The story-tellers knew that they were contributing to an artistic outcome, and one which would be widely seen, and most people were proud of their involvement. There would always be a performance offered in the venues where the interviews had been conducted. It was clear on these occasions that there was a strong sense of ownership on the part of the older people who had given their memories during the group and individual sessions. They saw that their particular interview had become part of a woven tapestry of stories reflecting a wide range of representative experience. In most cases they heard their actual words, taken from the interview, used verbatim in the theatre script. There were always comments like 'That's my story' or 'I told them that', indicating pride in their role in the project. There were occasional misunderstandings when someone felt that their story had been 'told wrong', perhaps if it was incomplete or if it was put together with a related story from someone else, but this was a rarity. Mostly, there was a strong sense of identification with the end-product on the part of the older contributors, even in cases where the writer and actors had developed a non-verbatim play more loosely based on the material collected.

RAISING AUDIENCE EXPECTATIONS

The interviewees mostly relished the idea that the resulting theatre productions would be performed by professional actors to other older people in homes, day centres and community centres, with the intention of providing relevant entertainment of a high artistic standard. The fact of professional actors being involved was very surprising to many of the story-tellers, and I think it made them feel that their contribution was going to get a good delivery and hearing.

It was interesting that the audiences too found it hard to believe that the players were professional, not because they were not excellent, but because they were used to much more amateur entertainment if any and were surprised they were getting 'the real thing'. All the music in the shows (which was always related to the theme and period covered in the play and therefore full of associations for the audiences) was played live by the actors on portable instruments (piano, drums, violin, oboe, clarinet, saxophone, bass, guitars, ukulele, etc.) and sung in harmony, which gave the shows terrific impact in smallish lounges of homes and day centres. Older people were always saying to the actors: 'You should be in the West End. It's better than anything on the telly.' This could be slightly frustrating for some actors, who took the work very seriously, but mostly they accepted these comments for the praise they really were. They pointed out in response that by performing in day-care and residential settings they could meet audiences for whom the plays had a particular meaning and who would relate to the material in a different way from a conventional theatre audience.

PERFORMANCE AS A STIMULUS FOR FURTHER REMINISCENCE

The performances of the plays had an additional agenda. They were designed to reflect the experiences shared in the interviews with many different audiences in the hope of triggering their memories and then sharing them with one another. This was sometimes achieved informally with the actors sitting with them and chatting over a cup of tea, or more formally in a structured reminiscence session led by one of the actors or the director after the performance. The actors were so close physically to their audience that they could see who was responding particularly strongly to their 'character' or to what was being said, and they were mostly intrigued enough to seek people out after the show and ask them what was behind the particular smile or tear they had noticed. The intimacy between actors and elders was a special element during the performances and in the post-show discussions at the different venues, and many actors set a high store on having this direct contact, so rare for performers who usually have the 'fourth wall' and a row of lights between them and their audience.

OLDER PEOPLE PERFORM THEIR OWN MEMORIES

Over the last 17 years I have been developing other forms of reminiscence theatre wherein the older people have performed their own memories. Some of these productions have been inter-generational, so that the children would play the older people when young, and the older people would play the older characters.[6] More often, the older people would play all the ages and parts, developing through improvisation original scenes from one another's stories. One group of older people became a semi-permanent group performing under the name 'The Good Companions', inspired by J.B. Priestley's novel about a group strolling players, which most of them had come across. The Good Companions would work with me over a three-month period meeting once or twice a week to listen to one another's memories around our chosen topic and to put these stories 'on the floor' with added music of the time and illustrative actions. Some plays looked at specific themes, such as the groups' first experiences of working life, 'Work in Progress', but others took a broader canvas and looked back over their lifetimes, such as 'Our Century and Us',

---

[6] 'Grandmother's Footsteps' about the older people's memories of their own grandparents, and 'Cheers', based on their memories of being young in World War II were two examples of this genre.

their most ambitious work. This group were often invited to perform overseas, and so a great deal of movement and gesture was built into the shows to aid audience understanding, and the additional exercise this required was beneficial to the players who were all aged 65 to 85. There is not time here to explain the full process,[7] but the Good Companions and other groups who worked together in this way developed a very strong sense of identity (both personal and as a group) and demonstrated greatly increased confidence and even ability. A couple of quotations here will make the point:

> *Joan:* I have far more confidence. Even about putting pen to paper, which you never do, do you, unless you write a letter, but if you've got a tale, a story, and then you find that it's accepted and put in a play or in a book, or in a newsletter that's for somebody to read, that gives you a lot of confidence.

> *Anne:* My great-granddaughter, Chloe, said 'Ooh Nanny, you'll be famous, you will!' She listens in to everything, she's only five-and-a-half, but she listens in! When I had to get my photographs done for the passport, there was a lady sitting in the photo booth, (she had to get a new bus pass because she'd had her handbag taken) and she wasn't sure of putting the money in, so the lady said to me, 'Oh you go in and do it first and I'll watch.' Chloe says to her, 'My Nan don't want photos for a bus pass, she wants to go to Germany, she's going in a show!' What could you do? (laughter) Talk about showing you up!

Much of the reminiscence theatre work involving older people performing has been with ethnic elders. It has helped in the consolidation of local community groups from a particular background, for example Nigerian, Caribbean, Irish, to build up confidence and increase their sense of being valued members of the wider community. A group of African elders from the Ajoda group in

---

7   For a longer description of the creative process, see P. Schweitzer, *Reminiscence Theatre: Making Theatre from Memories* published by Jessica Kingsley, 2007, chapters 7–9.

Woolwich put it into these words sent in a letter after creating the play:

> Working as a group on the play 'The Place Where I Grew Up', we all felt the scales were being removed from our eyes. It was like a tonic for us, making us feel strong and vigorous, and full of well-being as a group. As we shared memories of our school days and our other experience in common, there was a spirit of togetherness and unity of spirit which we had not found as a group before. The collective ideas which we generated during the work made the end result look like a purpose-written play. By being in touch with our shared history, members were lifted out of isolation and depression to a new sense of vitality. The play activated, motivated and stimulated us, triggering the spirit of acting which is generally found in every African heart.[8]

ADAPTING REMINISCENCE WHEN WORKING WITH PEOPLE WITH DEMENTIA

Over the last ten years, I have been exploring reminiscence in the context of dementia care through co-ordinating a Europe-wide project entitled 'Remembering Yesterday, Caring Today'. The project is aimed at families coping with dementia at home, and is supported by local dementia services health workers as well as arts-based session leaders with experience in working with dementia. The interview plays a lesser role here, as verbal communication can be problematic for people with dementia. Instead, the emphasis is on small group activity around a different theme each week, supported by a range of multi-sensory stimuli such as objects, images, sounds and tastes to trigger spontaneous memories. Stories emerging in the small groups, with support from professional group leaders, volunteers and family carers, are then shared with the wider group and explored through dramatic improvisation, song, dance, drawing and writing as well as straightforward discussion (Schweitzer and Bruce 2008). Dramatic

---

[8] See P.K. Schweitzer, *Mapping Memories: Reminiscence with Ethnic Minority Elders,* published by Age Exchange, London, 2004 for a fuller account of this work.

improvisation has been especially effective in transporting people with dementia back into long-ago situations and stimulating verbal recall and the capacity to replay the past with others. They are given plenty of time and encouragement to enable them to participate fully in what are usually highly sociable sessions.

Non-verbal exploration of memories and past skills and interests has the effect of activating and lifting the spirits of the participants and offering them ways of engaging with others, thus combating the frequent bouts of depression and sense of isolation associated with the onset of dementia. Such activities also remind the family carers that there are still many ways to reach their person, even where finding the words to express themselves is becoming increasingly difficult. In a recent Medical Research Council funded study of this project, one of the significant findings was that the autobiographical memory of people with dementia improved as a result of the intervention and another significant finding was that the carers' stress was reduced and their sense of hopefulness increased.[9]

SOME PERSONAL REFLECTIONS TO CONCLUDE

Having now reached the age of some of my younger interviewees, I have been thinking even more personally about the interview process and the effect of recalling earlier incidents individually and with groups.

Four years ago, on my 60th birthday, I left my place of work. It was my decision to stop at that point as I did not wish to become completely burnt out by the demands of my job and I wanted to try new things, do more free-lance directing and have some time for my grandchildren. Age Exchange was not just a work place for me. It had been my life for over 20 years and had absorbed every waking moment and lots when I should have been sleeping. My family had been dragged into helping me with it and listening to me talking about it ad nauseam and my husband had built parts of its base, the Reminiscence Centre and Bakehouse Theatre, in Blackheath,

---

[9] Medical Research Council funded trial platform 2005–7 led by Bangor University Department of Psychology.

London, with his own hands. So my departure from it was inevitably going to be tricky.

The move from being part of the official working world with a salary, an office, an in-tray and responsibilities, to being 'just me working from home' was initially quite traumatic. Needless to say, I did not do all those things we advise everyone retiring to do, like planning, preparing and clearing papers and building in a real break or holiday, despite having run a well-established pre-retirement project for 20 years for the benefit of others! Instead, I worked up to the last day, and well beyond, finishing projects.

I decided to write a book about my work in reminiscence theatre to get it out of my system and luckily was commissioned to do so. I found I could only do this through interview. The blank page terrified me, so I got a playwright friend to interview me over several weeks, amounting to about 24 hours of interview in total. The interviews were transcribed and I wrote the book from those transcripts. In this way, I was mirroring some of the processes I had used before with others. I tried to be honest and told about some of the awful times there had been as well as the good ones and some of the memories were painful, but the process of recall helped me to see the work as a whole and to feel some pride in it (Schweitzer 2007). It was satisfying to see parts of my life written down, even though it was really difficult honing the recorded transcribed text and deciding what to leave out. I think it has been a kind of stock-taking which makes it easier to move into the next period of my life as an independent freelance worker and consultant, with no base other than my own home.

Having more time at my disposal, I also had more chance to talk to the older people I had worked with over so many years and to reminisce with them about projects we have done together. Hearing their angles on the things we did, and hearing about some things they remember which I had completely forgotten, or even never knew about, triggered many memories and proved immensely enjoyable. It helped me see that the work we did together was remembered and valued. Reminiscence with others helped me to remind myself who I am, what I have done, who has been doing it with me and that it had made a difference. As a result of this experience, I am now developing

75

with partners in the European Reminiscence Network a new project around transitions in later life, which will use reminiscence and improvised theatre to explore subjectively the important issues of identity and ageing.

THE 'ORAL HISTORY' EXPERIENCE

Recently, I was interviewed by the Oral History Society about my life, and not just my work. I found this a very strange experience, especially as we ran out of time after four hours and the interview ended with a rather vague promise that it could perhaps be continued at a future date if extra time and money was available to cover the costs. I had enjoyed the process, though was foxed by some of the questions and uncertain of the value or interest of my answers to anyone else. I worried about some of the personal things I had said. I immediately wanted to have the interview set aside for a few years so any dust could settle or I wouldn't be around to see or hear any ructions it might cause. And I felt that if I had given the interview two days later, when not recovering from a nasty cough, I would have given a very different story. Aside from the factual information I shared, the gloss I put on such facts and recalled real-life events would have been very different. I felt there was something uncomfortably random in the apparent definitiveness of the version, which will be lodged in the Sound Archive of the British Library.

The experience was unsettling and served to point up for me the differences and similarities between this sort of formal life history interview and the kind of informal reminiscence work I had been conducting over the years in order to make plays and books and exhibitions. The interviews I had conducted, whether with groups or individuals, had been for an artistic purpose and had focused on a particular area, with no claims to elicit any single contributor's ultimate life summary. The stories generated were fed into a multi-layered product in which each person's individual experience was reflected as part of the broader picture. My recent experience of the Life Story interview also contrasted with my experience of being interviewed for the book on Reminiscence Theatre over many weeks, during which time I was in a variety of moods and states of mind and physical health, which undoubtedly affected my retrospective view of whatever we were discussing on a particular day. During the writing and editing of the book from the transcripts I was able to take these fluctuations in mood, both positive and negative, into account in the final version. With the Life Story interview it is there and finished (or in my case unfinished until some time later when a further interview was arranged to 'complete' it) and it was a true version of what I said on that day. It would be a nuisance, to say the least, if I wanted to review and change it all retrospectively. Even though I might not identify with it at all six months from the recording date, and much less so a decade on, I had to sign it off as accurate and rule out this impractical possibility.

I have been reflecting on this and thinking that the processes of oral history and reminiscence are really more different than I had thought initially. Perhaps this is a rather controversial note to end on, but these are thoughts in progress, and are offered as food for further discussion.

REFERENCES

Schweitzer, P. (ed.) (1975) *TIE Scripts for Secondary Schools, Primary Schools and Infant Schools.* London: Methuen.

Schweitzer, P. (2004) *Mapping Memories: Reminiscence with Ethnic Minority Elders.* London: Age Exchange Publications.

Schweitzer, P.K. (2007) *Reminiscence Theatre: Making Theatre from Memories.* London and Philadelphia: Jessica Kingsley.

Schweitzer, P. and Bruce, E. (2008) *Remembering Yesterday, Caring Today.* London and Philadelphia: Jessica Kingsley.

ABOUT THE AUTHORS

Joanna Bornat is the first Professor of Oral History in the UK and joint editor of the Journal of the UK Oral History Society. At the Open University she worked on reminiscence and life-history interviews, publishing extensively on the subject. A recent area of research involves re-analysing archived oral histories of the (mostly white) pioneers of geriatric medicine, and theorising on the problems of re-analysis in general. Joanna continues to be involved in community-based oral history projects.

Pam Schweitzer is a writer, theatre director, trainer and lecturer. In 1983, she founded Age Exchange Theatre Trust and was its Artistic Director until 2005. She has devoted the last 25 years to recording and preserving for posterity the memories of older people on key themes in the social history of the twentieth century. In 1993, Pam founded the European Reminiscence Network with partners in 16 European countries, and continues to co-ordinate and direct its projects.

Graham Smith is a Senior Lecturer in Oral History in the Department of History at Royal Holloway, University of London and before that was a lecturer in Healthcare Studies and Clinical Humanities in ScHARR at the University of Sheffield. He is currently Chair of the Oral History Society committee. His current research interests include the oral history of medicine and in particular memory and narrative.

Josie Tetley is a Senior Lecturer in Nursing at The Open University with specific responsibility for courses that focus on care work with older people. Josie is also committed to user participation in research. In order to engage people as fully as possible throughout her work she has used constructivist and narrative ways of working. Josie has been a member of the Centre for Biography and Ageing Studies at The Open University for the last two years.

Paul Thompson is a social historian and sociologist, internationally recognised as a pioneer of the use of oral history and life story interviews in social research. Paul is Emeritus Research Professor in Sociology at the University of Essex, author of over twenty books including *The Voice of the Past* and founder editor of the journal *Oral History*.

Alistair Thomson is an historian with a particular expertise in research and teaching using oral history and life history documents, including studies of migration, war and lifelong education. Previously Director of the Centre for Life History Research at Sussex University he returned to Australia in 2007 and is Professor of History at Monash University.